EL

# TOP 10
# ISTANBUL

MELISSA SHALES

D0431567

30289 418 1

## Top 10 Istanbul Highlights

## The Top 10 of Everything

DK | Penguin Random House

# CONTENTS

## Istanbul
## Area by Area

## Streetsmart

Within each Top 10 list in this book, no hierarchy of quality or popularity is implied. All 10 are, in the editor's opinion, of roughly equal merit.

***Front cover and spine*** *The domes of Hagia Sophia facing the Blue Mosque*
***Back cover*** *Cityscape of Istanbul with Süleymaniye Mosque and part of Golden Horn*
***Title page*** *Interior of Sultanahmet Mosque*

# Welcome to
# Istanbul

Istanbul is unique. No other city straddles two continents. No other city has been capital of two mighty empires. Its venerable churches, mosques and palaces do justice to its incredible past. This teeming metropolis of 14 million has a vibrant present, too, as a hotbed of the arts, and a shoppers', clubbers' and foodies' paradise. Explore it all with Eyewitness Top 10 Istanbul.

The city is defined by the sea. Imagine yourself on a ferry, hopping across the continent-dividing **Bosphorus Strait** for lunch in Asia; gazing out from the rooftop of your Sultanahmet hotel to the coruscating Sea of Marmara; or on a ferry up the **Golden Horn**, watching the exotic mosque-filled skyline of the Old City unfold. Istanbul is a city of contrasts, too. The ancient cathedral of **Haghia Sophia** is breathtaking; so is the ultra-cool **Istanbul Modern** gallery. Wander the backstreets of devout Fatih among bearded acolytes from the *medreses* by day; at night sip a cocktail in a chic rooftop bar in **Beyoğlu**, the heart of modern European Istanbul.

It isn't just the Bosphorus that divides Istanbul. The **Old City** sits on a hilly peninsula pointing at Asia. Here, Byzantine monuments, Ottoman mosques, historic markets such as the **Grand Bazaar**, and venerable **Turkish baths** predominate. Across the Golden Horn in Galata and Beyoğlu, three million shoppers, diners, and bar and gallery hoppers throng the main thoroughfare, **İstiklal Caddesi**, on any given weekend. Hip Istanbulites party here until 6am.

Whether you're here for a weekend or a week, our Top 10 guide will introduce you to the cream of everything the city has to offer. It is full of tips, from what to do for free to finding those off-the-beaten-track gems. With eight, easy-to-follow itineraries, **Top 10 Istanbul** will ensure you maximize your valuable time. Throw in handy maps and top-notch photographs and you have the ideal guide to one of the world's truly great cities. **Enjoy the book, and enjoy Istanbul.**

Clockwise from top: **Haghia Sophia, Blue Mosque, Basilica Cistern, Rumeli Hisari Fortress, Eyüp Sultan Mosque, the Galata Tower and Golden Horn, Great Palace Mosaic Museum**

# Exploring Istanbul

With so much to see and do in this continent-straddling city, it's sometimes hard to know where to begin. In order to help you make the most of your time, here are a few ideas for two and four days of sightseeing in Istanbul.

**Haghia Sophia**'s massive dome is considered to be the epitome of Byzantine architecture.

## Two Days in Istanbul

### Day ❶
**MORNING**

Admire the soaring dome and glittering mosaics of **Haghia Sophia** *(see pp16–17)*, then head off to explore the vast **Blue Mosque** *(see pp18–19)*.

**AFTERNOON**

Visit the sprawling **Topkapı Palace** *(see pp12–15)*, the nerve-centre of the Ottoman Empire. Afterwards relax in the **Çemberlitaş Baths** *(see pp30–31)*.

### Day ❷
**MORNING**

Explore the **Archaeological Museum** *(see pp20–21)*, full of artifacts from the Ottoman Empire's former domains.

**AFTERNOON**

Stroll to the top of the Old City's third hill to the **Süleymaniye Mosque Complex** *(see pp26–7)*, which offers views of the Bosphorus from its terrace. Then head back down to the bustling **Grand Bazaar** *(see pp22–3)* to weave through its 4,000 shops.

## Four Days in Istanbul

### Day ❶
**MORNING**

Spend most of the morning in the Byzantine cathedral of **Haghia Sophia** *(see pp16–17)*, before descending into the eerie depths of the **Basilica Cistern** *(see p63)*.

**AFTERNOON**

Catch a ferry up the Golden Horn to Ayvansaray and walk the line of the **Theodosian Walls** *(see p77)* to the fresco-filled wonder of the **Church of St Saviour in Chora** *(see pp28–9)*. Recover in the steaming **Çemberlitaş Baths** *(see pp30–31)*.

### Day ❷
**MORNING**

Start fresh in the airy courtyards and pavilions of the **Topkapı Palace** *(see pp12–15)* before walking across Sultanahmet Meydan park to the nearby **Blue Mosque** *(see pp18–19)*. Lunch in a tradesman's cafe in the **Grand Bazaar** *(see pp22–3)*.

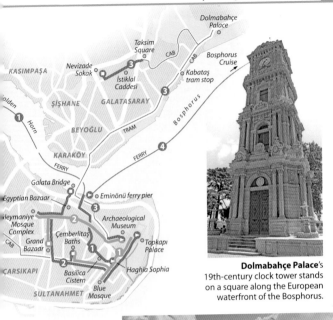

**Dolmabahçe Palace**'s 19th-century clock tower stands on a square along the European waterfront of the Bosphorus.

**Key**

— Two-day itinerary
— Four-day itinerary

The bustling **Eminönü waterfront** viewed from the Galata Bridge.

**AFTERNOON**

After exploring the bazaar, walk up to Süleymaniye Mosque Complex *(see pp26–7)* then down to the **Egyptian Bazaar** *(see pp70–71)* and **Eminönü** *(see p70)* waterfront. Lunch on a fish sandwich by **Galata Bridge** *(see p70)*.

## Day ❸
**MORNING**

Enjoy the splendours of the **Archaeological Museum** *(see pp20–21)* before taking a tram across the Golden Horn to Kabataş, then a cab or bus to the opulent, Baroque-style **Dolmabahçe Palace** *(see pp32–3)*, home to the later Ottoman sultans.

**AFTERNOON**

After exploring Dolmabahçe Palace, take a cab up to **Taksim Square** *(see p84)*. Walk down the city's premier shopping and entertainment street, **İstiklal Caddesi** *(see p86)*, and enjoy a meal at a lively *meyhane* (tavern) on **Nevizade Sokak** *(see p89)*.

## Day ❹
**ALL DAY**

Around 10:30am, depart from the Eminönü waterfront on the all-day **Bosphorus Cruise** *(see pp34–5)*. Enjoy fantastic views of the city's shoreline before lingering over a fish lunch in **Anadolu Kavağı** *(see p94)*.

# Top 10 Istanbul Highlights

The monumental Byzantine church
of Haghia Sophia

# 🔟 Istanbul Highlights

Istanbul is one of the greatest cities the world has ever known. Inhabited for at least 8,000 years, it was capital of two of the world's most powerful empires – those of the Byzantines and the Ottomans – and its every stone is steeped in history. The highlights are easy; you can cover the major attractions in the first couple of days. But after that, the choice can be overwhelming, especially as this ancient city is reinventing itself once more as a modern centre for nightlife, food and shopping. The only answer is to come back again and again to this endlessly fascinating city.

### ❶ Topkapı Palace

A palace fit for a sultan, the Topkapı was not only a royal residence, but also the Ottoman Empire's centre of government (see pp12–15).

### ❷ Haghia Sophia

One of the most revered icons of the Christian church, Haghia Sophia has stood for 1,500 years – a miraculous feat of design and engineering that has outlived two great empires (see pp16–17).

### ❸ Blue Mosque

Sultan Ahmet I's stunningly impressive mosque is one of the world's most famous religious buildings. "Blue" on account of the delicately patterned İznik tiles that adorn the interior (see pp18–19).

### ❹ Archaeological Museum

Turkey's world-class national collection contains ancient treasures from across the Ottoman Empire and beyond, including artifacts from Babylon, Syria, Egypt, Greece, Rome and Persia (see pp20–21).

### Süleymaniye Mosque Complex ⑥

Sultan Süleyman I built this magnificent mosque to glorify Allah and his own rule. The architect was the exceptional Sinan, who designed over 400 buildings throughout the empire *(see pp26–7)*.

### ⑤ Grand Bazaar

The Grand Bazaar remains a true Turkish delight, a shopaholic's fantasy that is also a photographer's dream *(see pp22–3)*.

### ⑦ Church of St Saviour in Chora

With more than 100 beautiful early-14th-century mosaics and frescoes, this church is one of the city's most important Byzantine treasures *(see pp28–9)*.

### Çemberlitaş Baths ⑧

Relaxing beneath the marble domes of these traditional baths offers a cleansing, cultural and reviving experience *(see pp30–31)*.

### ⑨ Dolmabahçe Palace

This 19th-century Occidental fantasy was commissioned by Sultan Abdül Mecit. The decision to build a lavishly opulent palace almost bankrupted the Treasury, and in the end could be financed only by foreign loans *(see pp32–3)*.

### ⑩ Bosphorus Cruise

Take to the water on a ferry trip up the Bosphorus. The air is clean, the pace unhurried and, best of all, sightseeing can be done from the deck *(see pp34–5)*.

# TOP 10 ⭐ Topkapı Palace

Fresh from his conquest of Constantinople, Mehmet II built Topkapı Sarayı as his main residence between 1460 and 1478. He planned it as a series of pavilions in four courtyards – a tribute in stone to the tent encampments of his nomadic forebears. Mehmet's palace was also the seat of government, and had a college for training officials and soldiers. While government moved across the road to the Sublime Porte in the 16th century, Topkapı continued as the sultan's palace until Abdül Mecit I moved to Dolmabahçe Palace in 1856.

### 1 Imperial Gate
(Bâb-ı Hümayun)
Built in 1478, this gate is the main entrance to the palace, with gate-keepers' quarters on either side. An apartment belonging to Mehmet II above the gate was destroyed by fire in 1866.

Topkapı Palace

### 2 Harem
A maze of rooms and corridors **(above)**, the Harem was a closed world occupied by the sultan's wives, concubines and children.

### 3 First Courtyard
(Alay Meydanı)
This vast outer courtyard takes in Gülhane Park, Sirkeci, the church of Haghia Eirene (Aya İrini Kilisesi) and the imposing Archaeological Museum.

### 5 Kitchens
These huge kitchens once catered for 1,000 people a day. On display is a collection of ceramics **(left)**, crystal and silver, including the Chinese celadon ware favoured by early sultans.

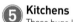

### 6 Throne Room
(Arz Odası)
In the Throne Room **(below)**, the Sultan would consult his ministers and governors, welcome ambassadors and other dignitaries, and host smaller state occasions.

### 4 Gate of Salutations
(Bâb-üs Selâm)
At this elaborate gate **(left)**, built in 1524, visitors were greeted, and high officials who had upset the sultan were arrested and beheaded. The gateway leads into the Second Courtyard (Divan Meydanı), where the Treasury now has a magnificent display of arms and armour.

**Entrance**

## RELIGIOUS RELICS

The Pavilion of the Holy Mantle (Has Oda Koğuşu) contains several of Islam's holiest relics. Exhibits include hairs from the Prophet's beard, one of his teeth, two of his swords and the sacred standard used during his military campaigns. The most important relic of all is the Holy Mantle, a plain black camel-hair cloak that the Prophet gave as a present to a poet. Once a year, it was displayed to high officials then doused in water; the drops squeezed from it were sent out as talismans against the plague.

### ⑩ Imperial Sofa
(Sofa-ı-Hümayun)

The Imperial Sofa **(below)** was a place to relax, its gardens studded with pavilions built by successive sultans. The finest is the Baghdad Pavilion (Bağdat Köşkü).

### ⑦ Third Courtyard
(Enderûn Meydanı)

The Gate of Felicity (Bâb-üş Saade) leads to the Third Courtyard, containing the sultan's private quarters and those of the Harem's white eunuchs.

### ⑧ Imperial Wardrobe
(Seferli Koğuşu)

Fittingly, the Imperial Wardrobe is now the home of the costume museum, a sumptuous collection of some 3,000 elaborately embroidered royal robes.

### ⑨ Treasury
(Hazine Koğuşu)

With exhibits including the jewel-encrusted Topkapı Dagger and the amazing 86-carat Spoonmaker's Diamond **(right)**, the Topkapı Treasury may be the most ostentatious collection of wealth ever gathered outside of the legendary Aladdin's cave.

## NEED TO KNOW

**MAP S3** ▪ Babıhümayun Cad
▪ (0212) 512 04 80
▪ www.topkapisarayi.gov.tr

**Open** *Palace:* Apr–Oct: 9am–7pm, Nov–Mar: 9am–5pm Wed–Mon. Adm: ₺30
*Harem:* Apr–Oct: 9am–7pm, Nov–Mar: 9am–4:30pm Wed–Mon. Adm: ₺15

*Haghia Eirene:* 9am–5pm. Adm: ₺20

▪ Expect long queues at the Pavilion of the Holy Mantle and Treasury.

▪ There is a restaurant, Karakol, (0212) 514 94 94, in the first courtyard, and another good restaurant, Konyalı, in the fourth. The latter is a good place to try Ottoman court cuisine, but it can be crowded. Book a table in advance on (0212) 513 96 96.

# Features of the Topkapı Harem

### 1 Barracks of the Black Eunuchs

Apart from the sultan and his sons, the only men allowed into the Harem were the black eunuchs, up to 200 slaves from Sudan and Ethiopia. Their barracks lie on one side of the Courtyard of the Black Eunuchs, with its arcade of marble columns.

**Courtyard of the Concubines**

### 2 Courtyard of the Concubines

This colonnaded courtyard lies beside the Harem Baths. As many as 300 concubines lived in the Harem at any one time.

### 3 Golden Cage

Mehmet III became sultan in 1595, following the murder of all but one of his 19 brothers. After that, heirs to the throne were kept in the "Golden Cage", a secure area of the Harem, until they were needed. As a result, many were weak and ill-fitted for rule when they took the throne.

### 4 Wives' Apartments

The sultan's wives (under Islamic law, he was allowed four) also had their own apartments. While wives took formal precedence in the Harem hierarchy, the real power lay with the sultan's favourites and mother. Occasionally, a sultan would marry a concubine – as in the case of Süleyman I, who married his beloved Roxelana (known in Turkish as Haseki Hürrem).

### 5 Salon of the Valide Sultan

The *valide sultan* (sultan's mother) was by far the most powerful woman in the palace, and enjoyed the use of some of the best rooms in the Harem.

### 6 Sultan's Apartments

The sultan spent much of his off-duty time in his suite within the Harem. Look out for the gilded bedroom of Sultan Abdül Hamit I (1774–89), the Hall of Murat III (1574–95) and the beautiful Fruit Room.

### 7 Imperial Baths

Next to each other at the centre of the complex are the baths of the sultan and the *valide sultan*, both elegantly faced with marble.

### 8 Imperial Hall

In the Imperial Hall, the sultan entertained his closest friends. Although the hall was within the Harem, only a few women – the sultan's mother, chief wife, favourites and daughters – were allowed entry.

### 9 Favourites' Apartments

*Haseki* (favourites) who bore a child received their own apartments and their freedom (if slaves). After the sultan's death, those who had borne only daughters were married out of the Harem or moved to the old palace; those with sons stayed in the palace.

**Favourites' Apartments**

### 10 Golden Way

This long, dark passage was so called because, on festivals, the Sultan would scatter gold coins here for the members of the Harem.

## LIFE IN THE HAREM

Behind the doors of the Harem, life was far less exciting than it was portrayed to be in the breathless accounts of 19th-century European commentators. There was undoubtedly intrigue and, if a woman was fortunate enough to be one of the sultan's favourites, she might well develop a taste for lavish comfort and lovely gifts, yet daily existence for most was mundane – even dully routine. The Harem was less a den of vice than a family home and girls' school. Of its 1,000 or so occupants, more than two-thirds were servants or royal children, while concubines – who usually arrived between the ages of 5 and 12 – spent years living in dormitories and undergoing a thorough education before being introduced to the sultan.

**Princess Mihrimah (1522–78), daughter of Süleyman I**

**TOP 10 OTTOMAN WOMEN**

**1 Hafsa Sultan** (mother of Süleyman I)

**2 Roxelana** (wife of Süleyman)

**3 Nurbanu Sultan** (wife of Selim II, daughter-in-law of Süleyman)

**4 Mihrimah** (daughter of Süleyman, wife of Grand Vizier Rüstem Paşa)

**5 Safiye Sultan** (mother of Mehmet III)

**6 Handan Sultan** (wife of Mehmet III)

**7 Kösem Sultan** (wife of Ahmet I)

**8 Turhan Hatice Sultan** (mother of Mehmet IV)

**9 Nakşidil Sultan** (mother of Mahmut II)

**10 Bezmialem** (wife of Mahmut II, mother of Abdül Mecit I)

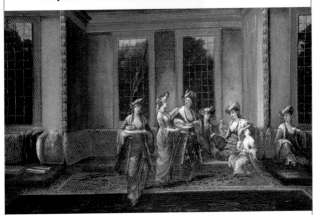

*Women Drinking Coffee* (1720s), by Jean-Baptiste Vanmour, is part of a collection of European art depicting life in the Harem. It is on display in the Pera Museum (*see p44*).

# TOP10 ⭐ Haghia Sophia

Haghia Sophia, the Church of Holy Wisdom (Ayasofya in Turkish), is an awe-inspiring expression of religious faith and one of the world's foremost architectural wonders. The first church on the site burned down in 404, the second was destroyed during the Nika Riots of 532, but the third – inaugurated by Emperor Justinian in 537 – stands firm today, despite countless wars and earthquakes, a blazing beacon to the faith of its creators. The church was converted into a mosque in 1453. Since 1935, it has been a museum.

## 1 Exterior

Its deep red walls are surmounted by a central dome and flanked by two semidomes on both sides. The main building is much as it was in the 6th century – except for the buttresses added to secure the structure, which, unfortunately, partly obscure the original shape **(right)**.

## 2 Galleries

Women used the galleries for prayer. There are splendid votive mosaics in the south gallery: look out for Christ Pantocrator (Almighty) with John the Baptist and the Virgin Mary; and Jesus Christ flanked by Empress Zoe and Emperor Constantine IX Monomachus **(below)**.

## 4 Weeping Pillar

Emperor Justinian rested his aching head against the damp stone of this pillar and was instantly cured. Ever since, visitors have queued to touch the miraculous spot.

## 5 Columns

The Byzantines were great scavengers, and many of the columns in the Haghia Sophia were probably salvaged from pagan temples.

## 3 Narthex

There are doors leading into the nave from each bay of the narthex; the large central one, the Imperial Gate, was once reserved for the emperor and the patriarch. At the south end of the narthex, look back above the door as you exit into the Vestibule of the Warriors to see the wonderful late 10th-century mosaic of Constantine and Justinian offering their city and church to the infant Christ.

### CHANGING FACES

In the last bay of the south gallery, look for the mosaic of Christ enthroned, flanked by Empress Zoë and Emperor Constantine IX Monomachus. The emperor's head has been altered. Historians believe that the figure was initially a portrait of Zoë's first husband, Romanos III Argyros, but was replaced with the image of her second husband, Michael IV, then the face of her third husband, Constantine.

### 6 Islamic Elements
The conversion from church to mosque began in 1453. Many of the mosiacs were plastered over, to be rediscovered in the 1930s. The *mihrab* and *minbar* (see p19) were added by Sultan Murat III in the 16th century. Note the calligraphic roundels **(left)** at the dome base.

### 7 Nave
On entering the nave **(below)**, the overwhelming impression is of the vast space enclosed by the dome. This sits on four arches rising out of four enormous marble piers, which frame double colonnades at either end.

### 8 Coronation Square
Set into the floor near the *minbar*, the site of the emperor's throne is marked in a square of patterned marble. In Byzantine times, this was thought to be the centre of the world *(omphalion)*.

### 9 Dome
The soaring dome **(left)**, 32 m (101 ft) in diameter, rises 56 m (183 ft) above the ground. Supported by 40 ribs made from lightweight hollow bricks, it is a miracle of engineering. The original design survived for 21 years before being destroyed by an earthquake in 1558.

### 10 Carpet Museum (Vakıflar Halı Müzesi)
Behind Haghia Sophia is the old soup kitchen, which today houses some of the country's oldest and finest mosque carpets.

**NEED TO KNOW**

**MAP R4** ■ Sultanahmet Meydanı ■ (0212) 522 17 50 ■ www.ayasofyamuzesi. gov.tr

**Open** Daily: Apr–Oct: 9am–7pm; Nov–Mar: 9am–5pm

Adm ₺30

■ After your visit, it's well worth coming back at night to see the exteriors of both Haghia Sophia and the Blue Mosque *(see pp18-19)* floodlit.

■ No refreshments are provided within the complex, but there are many options in Divanyolu Caddesi, a couple of minutes' walk away.

# ★ Blue Mosque

Sultan Ahmet I was only 19 when he commissioned this superb mosque, known in Turkish as the Sultanahmet Camii. So great was his enthusiasm for the project that at times he even worked alongside his labourers. With his architect, Sedefkar Mehmet Ağa, he wanted to surpass the Süleymaniye Mosque Complex (the work of Ağa's teacher, Sinan) and Haghia Sophia. The result of their labours, completed in 1616, has become one of the most celebrated mosques in the world, known widely as the Blue Mosque because of the blue İznik tiles in the interior.

### The Setting **1**
To underline the supremacy of Islam over Christian Byzantium, the Blue Mosque **(right)** was built opposite Haghia Sophia **(left)**, on the site of the Byzantine royal palace.

### **2** Entrance
The mosque's main entrance is for practising Muslims only. Separate entrances for visitors of other faiths are around the side of the mosque.

### **3** Minarets
Legend has it that the sultan asked for a minaret capped with *altın* (gold), but the architect heard *altı* (six) minarets. The sultan was pleased – at that time no mosque apart from the great mosque in Mecca had six minarets.

### **4** Domes
Semidomes **(below)** surround the main dome, which is 23.5 m (77 ft) in diameter and 43 m (140 ft) high, and supported by four giant columns, each 5 m (16 ft) in diameter.

### **5** Courtyard
The huge courtyard **(below)**, which is faced with cool marble from the island of Marmara, has the same dimensions as the interior of the prayer hall. Look up for a splendid view of the mosque's cascade of domes and semidomes.

### **6** Ablutions Fountain
The fountain at the centre of the mosque's courtyard is no longer used for ritual ablutions. Instead, the faithful use taps ranged along the outside of the courtyard. Washing the face, arms, neck, feet, mouth and nose is seen as an integral part of the act of prayer.

### 7 Tiles

There are more than 20,000 blue İznik tiles (above) lining the mosque's interior walls. Supplying these tiles put severe pressure on the tile makers, and the sultan banned anyone else from placing orders until his was complete.

### 8 Minbar and Mihrab

At the front of the mosque are the *minbar* (below), the pulpit from which the imam delivers his sermons, and the *mihrab*, which is a niche that points towards Mecca.

**NEED TO KNOW**

**MAP R5** ▪ Sultanahmet Meydanı
▪ (0212) 458 49 83

**Open** 9am–7pm daily, except during prayers

Donations

▪ To avoid prayer times, make the mosque your first stop in the morning, or visit in the mid-afternoon.

▪ There are no places for refreshment inside the mosque complex, but Sultanahmet Square, Divanyolu Caddesi and the Arasta Bazaar offer plenty of possibilities.

### 9 Sultan's Loge

To the left of the *mihrab* is the galleried box where the sultan prayed. The loge's ceiling is painted with arabesque designs.

### 10 Carpets

The whole of the interior of the mosque is laid with a modern carpet. Mosques have always had carpets in order to cushion the knees and forehead during prayer time (left).

# 🔟 ⭐ Archaeological Museum

The national collection of one of the world's most ancient and enthralling countries naturally promises something special, and this fabulous museum does not disappoint. A world-class collection spanning 5,000 years, it was founded in 1881 by Osman Hamdi Bey, the son of a Grand Vizier, fuelled by the realization that European archaeologists and treasure hunters were walking off with much of the Empire's heritage. There are three sections: the main museum, the Tiled Pavilion (Çinili Köşk) and the Museum of the Ancient Orient.

### 1 Sidon Sarcophagi
Osman Hamdi Bey discovered this remarkable group of 5th- and 4th-century-BC sarcophagi in Sidon (modern-day Lebanon) in 1887.

### 4 Ishtar Gate
The Ishtar Gate, built by King Nebuchadnezzar II in 575 BC, was decorated with mosaic ceramic panels of dragons and bulls **(right)**. The Processional Way through the gate was lined with 120 lions.

### 5 Hattuşa Sphinx
This enigmatic 13th-century-BC stone feline was one of four discovered in the great Hittite city at Hattuşa (Boğazkale) in Anatolia.

### 2 Alexander Sarcophagus
Its high-relief frieze shows scenes of Alexander in battle against the Persians, but the Alexander Sarcophagus **(above)**, dating from the late 4th century BC, is in fact the tomb of King Abdalonymos of Sidon (died c.312 BC). Faint traces remain of the gaudy colour that would once have covered it.

**Key to floorplan**
- ▨ Third floor
- ▨ Second floor
- ▨ First floor
- ▨ Ground floor

### 3 Halikarnassos Lion
The tomb of King Mausolus was one of the seven wonders of the ancient world – this simple lion **(left)** is a surviving relic.

Entrance

### 6 Treaty of Kadesh

The world's oldest surviving peace treaty, carved in stone in 1269 BC, was agreed by Egyptian Pharaoh Ramses II and King Hattusili III of the Hittites after a battle in present-day Syria. It lays out the terms of the ceasefire and agrees the safe return of refugees.

**ANCIENT WELCOME**

Visitors are greeted by an eclectic assortment of archaeological artifacts. In the entrance hall to the main museum stands a statue of the Egyptian god Bes. At the foot of the stairs to the Museum of the Ancient Orient are two basalt lions from Samal, dating from the 8th century BC. Outside the main museum are porphyry sarcophagi, from the 4th–5th century AD, thought to be those of Byzantine emperors. The portico itself is modelled on the 4th-century-BC Sarcophagus of the Mourning Women.

### 9 Museum of the Ancient Orient

This museum (right) has well-preserved exhibits from Mesopotamia, Egypt and Babylon, including some of the world's first known writing – cuneiform clay tablets from 2700 BC.

### 10 Tiled Pavilion

Built in 1472 as a sports pavilion (below), this is the oldest secular building in Istanbul. A masterpiece of İznik tiles itself, the pavilion also tells the interesting story of Turkish ceramics, with displays from İznik and Kutahya.

### 7 Istanbul Through the Ages

This thoughtful exhibit provides a fascinating insight into the city's history, with maps, plans and drawings alongside exhibits such as the original 14th-century bell from the Galata Tower.

### 8 Anatolia and Troy Gallery

Thousands of years of history (right) are imaginatively timelined in this long gallery. On one side you can travel through Anatolia from the Stone Age to the Iron Age. On the other, follow the history of Troy from 3000 BC to the 1st century AD.

**NEED TO KNOW**

**MAP S3** ■ Osman Hamdi Bey Yokuşu, Topkapı Sarayı, Gülhane ■ (0212) 520 77 40 ■ www.istanbularkeoloji.gov.tr

**Open** Daily: Apr–Oct: 9am–7pm; Nov–Mar: 9am–5pm

Adm ₺15

■ Due to ongoing earthquake proofing, some galleries are likely to be closed.

■ There is a small café in the grounds and a good souvenir shop next to it.

# 🔟 ⭐ Grand Bazaar

From the painted arches to the shopfronts gleaming with lanterns, piled with carpets or heaped with spices, the Kapalı Çarşı is a fantasy of Eastern opulence. Founded in 1461 by Sultan Mehmet II, the bazaar was designed as the trading heart of an empire. In addition to shops, banks, storerooms and cafés, it had mosques, travellers' accommodation, a bathhouse and a school. Destroyed several times by earthquake and fire, it has always bounced back. It offers a compelling and entertaining – if potentially expensive – day out.

**1 İç Bedesten**
This was the bazaar's first building **(right)**, a Byzantine structure converted in 1461 into a sturdy lock-up in which jewellery was traded and slaves were auctioned. Today, it is used to sell precious goods such as antiques and rare icons.

**2 Jewellers' Street**
(Kalpakçılar Caddesi)
The bazaar's widest street runs along the southern edge of the market, its shop windows piled high with jewels and precious metals. Some 100,000 kg (220,460 lb) of gold is traded in the bazaar each year **(right)**. Gold jewellery is sold by weight.

**5 Street Names**
At one time, each part of the bazaar had its own specialism, as indicated by the street names. Look for the *terlikçiler* (slipper-makers), *aynacılar* (mirror-makers), *fesçiler* (fez-makers), *yorgancılar* (quilt-makers), *kazazcılar* (silk-thread-makers) and *kürkçüler* (fur-makers).

**3 Carpet Sellers**
The bazaar is home to Istanbul's finest carpet dealers, as well as lesser traders keen to sell you a hall runner or a bedside rug. Shops are scattered throughout the market, especially near the İç Bedesten on Halıcılar Caddesi.

**4 Outdoor Stalls**
Surrounding the covered market is a maze of tiny lanes, with stalls selling carpets, souvenirs, clothes and vegetables. Locals shop here.

**6 Fountains**
Two marble and copper fountains provided drinking water for the market traders before modern plumbing was installed **(right)**. An 1880 survey noted there were also 16 drinking-water posts, one fountain reservoir and eight wells for firefighters.

### 7 Sandal Bedesten

In the southeast corner of the bazaar, the 15th-century Sandal Bedesten is the second oldest part of the bazaar. The roof of its arcade consists of 20 brick domes propped up by pillars. It is the former antiques market.

### 8 Gates

Twenty-two gates lead into the covered bazaar from all directions **(right)**. The Beyazıt Gate, rebuilt after an earthquake in 1894, is marked with the *tuğra* (imperial sign) of Sultan Abdül Hamit II, and the assurance that "God loves tradesmen".

### 9 Zincirli Han

The *hans* provided accommodation, food and stables for travelling traders. This one, the oldest of 40 in the area, has been lovingly restored and is now occupied by Şişko Osman, a leading carpet dealer.

### 10 Valide Han

Located on Mahmutpaşa Yokuşu, this huge building, constructed in 1651, has been sadly neglected. Today, it contains a mix of residential, gallery and workshop space.

---

**NEED TO KNOW**

**MAP N3** ■ www.grandbazaar istanbul.org.tr

**Open** 9am–7pm Mon–Sat (surrounding street markets are usually open longer and on Sun)

■ The hotels, school and bath-house that were once part of the bazaar have gone; now the market has a police station, ATM machines, public toilets and other necessities for keeping its droves of visitors happy.

■ There are small tea and coffee shops scattered throughout the market, as well as several good kebab shops, a couple of restaurants and a range of upmarket cafés.

---

**FACTS AND FIGURES**

The Grand Bazaar is one of the world's largest buildings, containing a network of 61 covered streets and enclosing an area of 307,000 sq m (3,305,000 sq ft). Every day in this teeming marketplace, as many as 30,000 traders in 4,500 shops befriend and haggle with up to 400,000 shoppers – both locals and visitors from all around the world. In business since its foundation in 1461, the bazaar is the world's oldest covered market.

---

*Following pages* Vast nave of the Haghia Sophia

# TOP10 ⭐ Süleymaniye Mosque Complex

One of the finest creations of the Ottoman Empire's greatest architect, Sinan, Süleymaniye Camii was built in 1550–57 for Süleyman I. This hilltop mosque was constructed as part of a charitable foundation *(külliye)*. The mosque's dome and minarets dominate the skyline in a matchless display of imperial power, while its delicate calligraphy, stained-glass windows and decorative carvings add a lightness of touch. Süleyman and his wife Roxelana are buried in tombs in the courtyard.

### 1 Mosque Interior

The interior is simple and serene. The blue, white and gold dome **(right)** contains 200 stained-glass windows. The *mihrab* and pulpit are made from white marble with İznik tiles.

### 2 Süleyman's Tomb

Sultan Süleyman I, "the Magnificent", lies in a grandiose garden tomb **(below)**, with an ebony, mother-of-pearl and ivory door and a dome inlaid with ceramic stars.

### 3 Sinan's Tomb

Sinan's mausoleum is on the site of the house he lived in when building the mosque, just beyond the northwest corner of the complex. It is a modest memorial to a prodigious talent.

### 4 Hamam

This mosque's *hamam* is a mixed-sex bathhouse, which makes it good for families. Somewhat alarmingly, it offers all visitors free life insurance during their bath!

### 5 Courtyard

This great courtyard **(right)** is surrounded by a colonnade of porphyry, Marmara and pink Egyptian columns, said to be recycled from the Hippodrome.

### 6 Medreses
Two of the six *medreses* (colleges) **(above)** – once part of the Imperial religious school providing theological and general education – house Süleyman's library of 110,000 manuscripts.

### 7 Addicts' Alley
The cafés of "Addicts' Alley", formally known as Prof Sıddık Sami Onar Caddesi, once sold opium and hashish. It still has its cafés, but now the drug of choice is tobacco smoked in a water pipe *(nargile)*.

**NEED TO KNOW**

**MAP M2** ■ Prof Sıddık Sami Onar Cad ■ (0212) 522 02 98

**Open** 9am–7pm daily (closed at prayer times); Süleyman's tomb open 9:30am–4:30pm; *hamam* open 7am–midnight daily

Adm charge for *hamam*

...........................................................

■ Take time out to admire some of the restored wooden houses in the nearby streets.

■ There are many refreshment options, with the Darüzziyafe Restaurant *(see p73)* in the old soup kitchen, the Lalezar Café and a row of cafés serving Turkish baked beans right opposite the main entrance to the complex.

### 8 İmaret
The mosque kitchens not only fed the many workers, students, teachers and priests in the complex **(left)**, but ran a soup kitchen for up to 1,000 people a day.

**SINAN**

The incomparable Mimar Sinan, builder of 146 mosques and over 300 other buildings, never trained as an architect. He was born Christian in 1489, and was conscripted to serve in the sultan's elite Janissary (New Army) Corps. He rose through the ranks to become Commander of the Infantry Cadet Corps, responsible for military engineering works, then in 1536 was appointed Architect of the Abode of Felicity by Süleyman. He held the post until his death, aged 99, in 1588.

### 9 Caravanserai
The mosque was a full-service complex – in the caravanserai, visitors could find food and lodging.

### 10 Views
The terraced gardens outside the main complex offer fine views **(below)** across the Golden Horn.

# TOP 10 ⭐ Church of St Saviour in Chora

The Church of St Saviour in Chora is home to one of the world's finest collections of Byzantine art: more than 100 magnificent mosaics and frescoes depicting biblical images. They were commissioned in 1315–21 by Byzantine statesman Theodore Metochites, who also restored the 11th-century church on the site. The church was converted into a mosque in 1511 and is known by locals as Kariye Mosque (Kariye Camii). Its works of art slipped into obscurity until they were rediscovered in 1860. Restoration began in 1948.

### Exterior ①

Walk round the back of the church **(right)** to experience the full impact of its architecture – masonry of striped marble, six domes, layers of arches, undulating rooflines and, to one side, a minaret.

### ② Genealogy of Christ

The two domes of the inner narthex (western entrance) portray 66 of Christ's forebears. In one dome **(above)**, the Virgin and Child survey the kings of the House of David. In the other, Christ is surrounded by ancestors including Adam, Abraham, Jacob and Jacob's 12 sons.

### ③ Anastasis Fresco

This resurrection fresco **(below)** depicts Christ pulling Adam and Eve from their graves, while the gates of hell are broken and Satan lies bound at Christ's feet.

### ④ Paracclesion

A funerary chapel south of the main church, this is a glory of frescoes depicting judgment and resurrection. The unmarked tomb in the north wall may be that of Theodore Metochites.

### ⑤ Ministry of Christ

The vaults of seven bays in the outer narthex and the south bay of the inner narthex detail the ministry of Christ, including his temptation and miracles such as healing of the sick.

**6 Mosaic of Theodore Metochites**

Over the door leading from the inner narthex to the nave is a superb mosaic **(left)** depicting Theodore Metochites in a large turban presenting his church to Christ, who raises a hand in blessing.

**7 The Last Judgment**

In the main dome of the Paracclesion is a vision of the Last Judgment, with Christ in Majesty flanked by the Virgin Mary, John the Baptist and the Apostles.

**8 Life of the Virgin**

Twenty mosaics **(right)** in the inner narthex depict the life of the Virgin Mary, based on the apocryphal 2nd-century Gospel of St James. They include images of Mary's first steps (at six months old).

**CHURCH GUIDE**

You now enter through a side door, but the main entrance was originally by way of a long porch, the outer narthex, which leads into an inner narthex. In the alcoves of these two porches you find the majority of the mosaics. The inner narthex opens into the main body of the church (the nave). At the far end, the altar stands in front of the semicircular apse, flanked by the Prothesis (Communion chapel) and Diakonikon (vestry). To one side is the Paracclesion.

**9 Infancy of Christ**

Scenes from Christ's infancy are depicted in the semicircular panels of the outer narthex. Based on New Testament accounts, they include the Journey to Bethlehem, Mary and Joseph enrolling for taxation, the Nativity, and the terrible Massacre of the Innocents.

**10 Dormition of the Virgin**

This beautiful mosaic in the nave **(below)** shows Christ sitting beside his mother's coffin, cradling a baby that represents her soul. Above is Ashrael, the Angel of Death.

**NEED TO KNOW**

**MAP B2** ■ Kariye Camii Sok, Kariye Meydanı, Edirnekapı ■ (0212) 631 92 41

**Open** 9am–5pm daily

Adm ₺15

■ Photography is permitted, but flash is forbidden.

■ The Asitane Restaurant next door (see p79) is a pleasant garden café, and one of the best places in Istanbul for traditional Ottoman cuisine.

# 🔟⭐ Çemberlitaș Baths

No stay in Istanbul would be complete without a bout of steaming, soaping, scrubbing and massaging in a Turkish bath *(hamam)*. Çemberlitaș, built in 1584, is commonly hailed as one of the most beautiful. Designed by Sinan, it was commissioned by Selim II's wife, Nurbanu Sultan, as a way of providing financial support for the Atik Valide Sultan Mosque in Üsküdar *(see p100)*, of which she was sponsor. Today, Çemberlitaș is still used by Turks, but is most popular with tourists and photographers – it's a regular location for film and fashion shoots.

### ❶ Entrance
At the ticket office, you are given a *peştemal* (a type of sarong, for modesty) **(below)**, a *kese* (a coarse mitt for scrubbing the body down) and tokens to give to the attendants. Men and women are then sent off to separate sections.

### ❷ Men's Section
Originally the *hamam* consisted of two identical suites of rooms, each with a separate entrance. The men's section of the baths is still exactly as envisaged by its creator, Sinan.

### ❸ Women's Section
The women's changing area was lost in 1868, when Divanyolu Caddesi was widened, so women now change in a corridor; but their hot room is unaltered.

### ❺ Hot Room (Sıcaklık)
The hot room has a domed ceiling supported by 12 arches that rise from marble columns **(above)**. The dome is pitted with glass "elephants' eyes", which channel the light through the steam to polka-dot the floor.

### ❹ Dressing Room
(Camekan)
In the dressing room **(above)**, an attendant will assign you a locker and give you a pair of slippers. Most people go nude under the *peştemal*, but wear a swimsuit if you wish to.

**Key**
- ▢ Men's section
- ▢ Women's section

### 6 Private Cubicles (Halvets)
Around the walls are a number of private cubicles with taps running cold, warm and hot water, which you can use to wash or cool down if the heat gets too much for you.

### 7 Navel Stone (Göbek Taşı)
In the centre of the hot room is a large slab of marble. Lie down and wait for the attendant. You will be covered in soap suds, and scrubbed all over with the *kese*. Then you will be lathered again, washed with a cloth, and soap-massaged **(below)**. Finally, your hair will be washed, and you will be vigorously rinsed with buckets of water.

### 8 Cool Room (Soğukluk)
The cool room is the place to sit and chat. The men's is as elegant as it was in Sinan's day; the women's is more modern. Afterwards, head back to change, or go for your oil massage.

### 9 Oil Massage Room
You will be one of several people being massaged **(below)** on a row of beds under bright lights. It's worth any discomfort you may experience – you'll feel great afterwards.

### 10 Extras
Take as much time as you like to return to the steam room or sit in the cool room. If you want the full works, the attendants will be happy to give you a manicure, pedicure or facial.

# 🔟 ⭐ Dolmabahçe Palace

In 1843, Sultan Abdül Mecit, who wanted to reinvent the Ottoman Empire in a European image, employed Armenian architects Garabet and Nikoğos Balyan to build a luxurious new palace on the Bosphorus shore. Dolmabahçe Sarayı, completed in 1856, is the result. Luxurious it certainly is, with 285 rooms and 43 reception halls, and lavish decoration in gold and crystal that rivals the Palace of Versailles in France. Ironically, this extravagance hastened the end of the Empire, and the last sultan fled from here into exile in 1922.

## Ceremonial Hall ❶
(Muayede Salonu)
The dome in this vast hall **(right)** is 36 m (118 ft) high. The Bohemian crystal chandelier, a gift from Queen Victoria of England, has 750 lights and weighs 4.5 tonnes (9,900 lb). It is the world's largest chandelier.

## ❷ Gates
The palace had two ceremonial entrances, both highly ornamented: the Treasury Gate, which is now the main entrance, and the Imperial Gate **(above)**. Both gates still have a guard of honour.

## ❸ Waterfront Façade
The marble façade **(below)** is 284 m (930 ft) long. The State Rooms are on the left, the Ceremonial Hall in the centre and the Harem on the right.

## ❹ Harem
The Harem has several apartments, furnished to various grades of luxury (for the sultan, his mother, wives, concubines, servants and guests) – also baths, a school, a maternity ward and a central salon where the wives and concubines would meet for tea.

## ❺ State Rooms (Selamlık)
The rooms on the palace's seaward side were used by the Grand Vizier and ministers, while those on the landward side were administrative offices. They are all lavishly decorated.

## ❻ Sultan's Bathrooms
The Sultan had two bathrooms: one in the main palace, faced in marble; the other in the Harem, decorated in violet flowers.

### 7 Crystal Staircase

The ornate staircase (above) has balusters of Baccarat crystal. It links the administrative offices with the ceremonial rooms upstairs.

### 8 Clock Tower

The four-storey tower, 27 m (90 ft) high, was added to the palace in 1890, during the reign of Sultan Abdül Hamit II (see p91). The clock – which still keeps time – was built by the celebrated Parisian clock-maker Paul Garnier.

### 9 Gardens

The palace and gardens (below) stand on reclaimed land (the name Dolmabahçe means "Filled Garden"). In addition to the palace and its 16 external pavilions, the grounds once held a flour mill, pharmacy, aviary, glass factory and foundry.

### ATATÜRK

Born in 1881, Mustafa Kemal rose to prominence in 1915, leading Turkish forces to victory at Gallipoli. A leader of the Young Turks republican movement, he seized his moment following the end of World War I, abolishing the sultanate in 1922 and declaring a republic in 1923. As Turkey's first president, he westernized the country – introducing the Latin alphabet, compulsory schooling and rights for women. He is still idolized as the "Father of the Turks" (Atatürk); it is illegal in Turkey to criticize him publicly.

### 10 Atatürk's Rooms

In the first years of the republic, Atatürk used the palace as his Istanbul base, keeping an office and bedroom (below) in the Harem. He died here, from cirrhosis of the liver, on 10 November 1938 – all the palace's clocks are set to 9:05am, the moment of his death.

### NEED TO KNOW

**MAP C5** ■ Dolmabahçe Cad ■ (0212) 236 90 00 ■ Tram: Kabataş, then a 5-minute walk
■ www.dolmabahce.gov.tr

**Open** 9am–4pm Tue, Wed & Fri–Sun (to 3pm Oct–Feb)

Adm ₺30 for Selamlık, ₺20 for Harem, ₺40 for a combined ticket

■ Admission to the palace is by guided tour only. There are two itineraries: one of the Selamlık (the areas reserved for men, including the Ceremonial Hall); the other of the Harem (including the living quarters of the royal women, the sultan's private quarters, and Atatürk's bedroom, bathroom and study).

■ There is a café in the Clock Tower, and toilets near both entrances.

# **TOP 10** ⭐ **Bosphorus Cruise**

The Istanbul skyline is justifiably one of the most famous cityscapes in the world and, while there are many places from which to admire it, by far the best is the deck of a boat on the Bosphorus. After the bustle of the city centre, a trip up the Bosphorus gives you an entirely different perspective on the city. Give your lungs a break from the traffic fumes and your feet a rest from trudging pavements. Take the local ferry for a modest fare, and spend a day floating serenely along the straits past magnificent shores and wooden villas.

### **1** Eminönü Pier
The Bosphorus ferry departs from Eminönü port **(above)**, the city's busiest ferry terminal. Pick up a *simit* or fish sandwich from a street vendor.

### **2** Leander's Tower (Kız Kulesi)
This tower, off the Üsküdar shore, is a restaurant. Its Turkish name means "Maiden's Tower", after a legendary princess kept there; the English name refers to a hero of Greek myth *(see p97)*.

### **3** Dolmabahçe Palace (Dolmabahçe Sarayı)
Sultan Abdül Mecit virtually mortgaged the Ottoman Empire to build this lavish, European-style palace in the 1850s.

### **4** Ortaköy
One of the prettiest villages on the straits, at the foot of the Bosphorus Bridge, Ortaköy **(below)** is a weekend retreat for İstanbulites.

### **5** Bosphorus Bridge (Boğaziçi Köprüsü)
Completed in 1973, this 1,510-m- (4,954-ft-) long bridge, stretching between Ortaköy and Beylerbeyi, was the first to link Europe and Asia.

---

**IT'S ALL A MYTH**

When Greek goddess Hera sent a swarm of gnats to plague the beautiful Io, her rival for the affections of the god Zeus, Io turned herself into a cow and swam across the straits to escape, giving the Bosphorus its name – the "Ford of the Cow". In another Greek myth, Jason and the Argonauts rowed up the Bosphorus in search of the Golden Fleece – perhaps an echo of the Black Sea tradition of using a lamb's fleece to trap gold when panning.

**6** **Beylerbeyi Palace (Asian Side)**
(Beylerbeyi Sarayı)
This fussy palace **(above)** was built as a summer annexe to the Dolmabahçe. It had no kitchens, and food was rowed across as required.

**9** **Sarıyer**
This village is the main fishing port on the Bosphorus. It has a historic fish market, as well as several good fish restaurants near the shore.

**10** **Anadolu Kavağı (Asian Side)**
This is the last stop for the ferry **(below)**, and the locals make a good living selling fish lunches and ice cream to tourists. The 14th-century Yoros Kalesi, a Genoese Castle, affords good views.

**7** **Arnavutköy and Bebek**
The pretty 19th-century wooden villas *(yalıs)* that line the waterfront along this central stretch of the Bosphorus are the city's most desirable real estate.

**8** **Fortress of Europe**
(Rumeli Hisarı)
This castle **(below)** was built by Mehmet the Conqueror in 1452 prior to his attack on Constantinople. Across the water stands the Fortress of Asia (Anadolu Hisarı), built in the late 14th century.

**NEED TO KNOW**

**MAP F4** ■ Departs from Eminönü Boğaz Hattı Pier ■ (0212) 444 18 51 ■ www.sehirhatlari.com.tr

Departures daily, May–Oct: 10:35am & 1:35pm; Nov–Apr: 10:35am

Fare ₺15 one way, ₺25 return

■ The return cruise takes around 6 hours, including a 2.5-hour lunch stop at Anadolu Kavağı. If you would like to visit any of the sights en route, take the ferry one way and return by bus. The bus, however, can be extremely slow.

■ Food is available on the ferry and there are various food facilities at the last stop in Anadolu Kavağı.

# The Top 10
# of Everything

Basilica Cistern, an underground water
reservoir constructed in the 6th century

# 🔟 Moments in History

**1** **AD 330–95: Division of the Roman Empire**

In 330, Constantine moved the capital of the Empire from Rome to the former Greek colony of Byzantium. It was initially called New Rome but later became Constantinople ("City of Constantine"). In 395, Theodosius divided the Empire between his sons, with the western half run from Rome and the eastern (Byzantine) half centred on Constantinople.

**Bust of Constantine**

**2** **1071: Battle of Manzikert**

The Seljuk Turks coming from Persia defeated Byzantine forces at Manzikert and seized most of Anatolia. The Byzantines never recovered their eastern lands.

**3** **1204: Sack and Capture of Constantinople**

The armies of the Fourth Crusade sacked Constantinople, driving the emperor into exile. Crusader rulers governed in Constantinople until 1261, when Byzantine Emperor Michael VIII Palaeologus recaptured the city.

**Capture of Constantinople in 1204**

**4** **1453: Conquest of Constantinople**

Following years of Ottoman encroachment into the Byzantine Empire, Sultan Mehmet II captured Constantinople, converting the church of Haghia Sophia into the mosque of Ayasofya. The last Byzantine emperor, Constantine XI, died fighting on the city walls.

**5** **1529: Siege of Vienna**

The Ottoman Empire reached its maximum extent under Süleyman I. In 1526, he had taken control of southern Hungary. In the spring of 1529, he mustered a huge military force with the aim of consolidating his Hungarian gains and moving on to Vienna. A combination of serious flooding en route and a spirited defence led by a German mercenary, Niklas Graf Salm, sent the Turks packing and marked the end of Ottoman expansion in Western Europe.

**6** **1777: Turkish Delight**

Ali Muhiddin Hacı Bekir, confectioner to the imperial court, invented a chewy sweet flavoured with rosewater and coated in icing sugar: *rahat lokum* ("morsel of contentment"), better known as Turkish delight.

**7** **1853–6: Crimean War**

When Russia began to encroach on Ottoman territory, Britain and France weighed in on the side of the Turks. Englishwoman Florence Nightingale set up a hospital in Istanbul, defining modern nursing practice *(see p97)*.

**Mustafa Kemal**

### 8 1919–23: Birth of the Republic

Mustafa Kemal – or Atatürk ("Father of the Turks") – led a bloodless revolution that abolished the sultanate, and fought a fierce war of independence. In 1923, as first president of the new Republic of Turkey, he moved the capital to Ankara, leaving Istanbul without political status for the first time in 1,600 years.

**Construction of the Bosphorus Bridge, 1972**

### 9 1973: Bosphorus Bridge

The Bosphorus Bridge was opened between Ortaköy and Beylerbeyi, linking European Turkey to Asian Anatolia.

### 10 2015: PM Erdoğan wins Fourth Term

The November 2015 elections saw the Justice and Development Party (AKP), win a fourth successive term in government, with almost 50 percent of the vote.

**TOP 10 NOTABLE OTTOMAN SULTANS**

**Sultan Mehmet II**

**1 Osman Gazi** (1299–1326)
The Ottoman dynasty takes its name from that of its founder, Osman. In 1301, his forces won the first Ottoman victory against the Byzantine Empire at the Battle of Baphaeon.

**2 Orhan Gazi** (1326–60)
Orhan moved the Ottoman capital to Bursa and established Islam as the state religion.

**3 Murat I** (1360–89)
Murat founded the Janissary Corps, an elite group within the Ottoman army.

**4 Mehmet II the Conqueror** (1451–81)
In 1453, Mehmet captured Constantinople from its Byzantine rulers. He laid out a new city on the rubble, and founded Topkapı Palace.

**5 Süleyman I the Magnificent** (1520–66)
A conqueror, lawmaker and patron of the arts, Süleyman presided over the golden age of Ottoman rule (see p62).

**6 Mehmet III** (1595–1603)
Mehmet's mother had 18 of his 19 brothers strangled so that he could take the throne.

**7 Osman II** (1618–22)
The Janissaries killed Osman at Yedikule after his failed attempt to curb their power.

**8 Mahmut II** (1808–39)
Mahmut wiped out the Janissary Corps, slaughtering thousands in the purge.

**9 Abdül Hamit II** (1876–1909)
Abdül Hamit built Yıldız Sarayı, the last of the imperial palaces.

**10 Mehmet VI** (1918–22)
The last of the Ottoman sultans fled into European exile in November 1922.

# 🔟 Byzantine Monuments

**Haghia Sophia as seen from Sultanahmet Square**

### 1 Haghia Sophia (Ayasofya)

Built by Emperor Justinian in the 6th century, Haghia Sophia is one of the world's greatest architectural achievements. Justinian was so proud of his basilica that he proclaimed: "Glory to God who has thought me worthy to finish this work. Solomon, I have outdone you" *(see pp16–17)*.

### 2 Hippodrome (At Meydanı)

Once a Byzantine race track 450 m (1,500 ft) long, the Hippodrome could hold 100,000 people. It was the scene of celebrations and, on occasion, bloodshed; the Nika Riots in 532 ended with 30,000 dead *(see p60)*.

### 3 Cisterns

To ensure good water supply in times both of peace and of siege, the Byzantines built a series of vast underground water cisterns beneath their city. The finest are the Basilica Cistern (Yerebatan Sarnıcı) *(see p63)* and the Cistern of 1,001 Columns (Binbirdirek Sarnıcı) *(see p64)*.

**The underground Basilica Cistern**

### 4 Church of St Saviour in Chora (Kariye Camii)

The main reason to visit this 11th-century Byzantine church is its glorious collection of mosaics and frescoes, which depict biblical scenes *(see pp28–9)*.

**Section of the Theodosian Walls**

### 5 Theodosian Walls (Teodos II Surları)

Over the course of 1,000 years, the curtain walls built by Emperor Theodosius II in 412–22 proved to be a necessity – they withstood more than 20 attacks by Huns, Arabs, Bulgarians, Turks and Russians, finally succumbing to the Ottomans in 1453 *(see p38)*. The walls have now been partially restored *(see p77)*.

### 6 Great Palace Mosaic Museum (Büyük Saray Mozaikleri Müzesi)

Only fragments remain of the Great Palace of the Byzantine emperors. This small museum houses one of them – the mosaic passageway, discovered in the 1930s, that led from the palace to the royal box in the Hippodrome. The beautifully crafted floor depicts wild animals and hunting scenes *(see p64)*.

### 7 Church of SS Sergius and Bacchus
(Küçük Ayasofya Camii)
In the historic heart of the city, just south of Sultanahmet Square, the Church of SS Sergius and Bacchus was built in the 6th century and has an original Greek frieze *(see p65)*.

### 8 Aqueduct of Valens
(Bozdoğan Kemeri)
This beautifully preserved 4th-century aqueduct, which remained in use until the 19th century, was a key part of the system that carried fresh water into the Byzantine capital from the forests of Thrace *(see p75)*.

### 9 Haghia Eirene
(Aya İrini Kilisesi)
One of the oldest churches in the city, Haghia Eirene stands in the outer courtyard of the Topkapı Palace. The church was rebuilt in the 6th century and acted as a sister church to the nearby Haghia Sophia. Today the church is open to the public and, because of its excellent acoustics, concerts are often held here *(see p65)*.

### 10 Church of the Pammakaristos
(Fethiye Camii)
This 12th-century Byzantine church served as the worldwide head-quarters of the Greek Orthodox faith during the 15th and 16th centuries. It was converted to a mosque in 1573. The former funer-ary chapel is now a museum housing magnif-icent mosaics *(see p75)*.

**Mosaic in the Church of the Pammakaristos**

## TOP 10 NOTABLE BYZANTINE RULERS

**Sovereign Theodora and Antonina**

**1 Constantine** (306–37)
Constantine moved the capital of the Roman Empire from Rome to Constantinople in 330 AD *(see p38)*.

**2 Theodosius II** (408–50)
Emperor Theodosius codified the law, founded a university and built the city walls *(see p77)*.

**3 Justinian I** (527–65)
Justinian founded many great buildings, including Haghia Sophia *(see pp16–17)*, as well as reforming the law.

**4 Theodora** (527–48)
A bear-keeper's daughter turned stripper and prostitute, Theodora ruled alongside her husband Justinian I.

**5 Justinian II** (685–95 and 705–11)
Justinian's enemies deposed him then cut off his nose, because a disfigured man could not be emperor. He later regained the throne wearing, it is said, a prosthetic nose of solid gold.

**6 Irene of Athens** (797–802)
Irene was the first woman to rule the Empire on her own.

**7 Basil I** (867–86)
The homosexual lover of Michael III, Basil was crowned joint emperor in 866, then killed Michael to rule alone.

**8 Zoë** (1028–50)
Zoë wed three times after becoming empress aged 50.

**9 Romanus IV Diogenes** (1067–71)
Romanus was defeated by the Seljuks at Manzikert in 1071 and as a result he was exiled.

**10 Constantine XI Palaeologus** (1449–53)
The last of the Byzantines died fighting on the city walls during the conquest of 1453.

# 🔟 Places of Worship

**Süleymaniye Mosque Complex**

### 1 Süleymaniye Mosque Complex
(Süleymaniye Camii)

This vast mosque *(see pp26–7)*, which dominates the skyline of the Golden Horn, is the crowning achievement of Koca Mimar Sinan, greatest of imperial architects. Built in 1550–57 in the grounds of the old palace, Eski Saray, it is a suitably grand memorial to its founder, Süleyman I *(see pp38–9 & p62)*.

### 2 Blue Mosque
(Sultanahmet Camii)

Commissioned by Sultan Ahmet I, the magnificent Blue Mosque was built by the imperial architect Sedefkar Mehmet Ağa, a pupil of the great Sinan, in 1609–16. The mosque takes its name from the blue İznik tiles that line its inner walls *(see pp18–19)*.

### 3 Fatih Mosque
(Fatih Camii)

The original Fatih Mosque was built by Mehmet II to celebrate his capture of Constantinople in 1453; its name means "the Conqueror's mosque". The present mosque was built in the 18th century by Mustafa III, after an earthquake in 1766 destroyed the original *(see p75)*.

### 4 Eyüp Sultan Mosque
(Eyüp Camii)

Also rebuilt after the 1766 earthquake, this mosque at the top of the Golden Horn is one of the holiest places in Islam. It is built around the tomb of a 7th-century saint, Eyüp el-Ensari, standard-bearer of the Prophet Mohammed *(see p76)*.

### 5 Atik Valide Mosque
(Atik Valide Camii)

One of Istanbul's finest mosques and Sinan's last great work, the "Old Mosque of the Sultan's Mother" was completed in 1583 for the formidable Nurbanu, wife of Selim III and mother of Murat III *(see p100)*.

**Elegant interior of the Atik Valide Mosque, Üsküdar**

### 6 Church of St George
(Ortodoks Patrikhanesi)

The Church of St George stands within the Greek Orthodox Patriarchate complex. Built in 1720, it includes a superb 11th-century mosaic of the Virgin Mary *(see p78)*.

### 7 Armenian Patriarchate
(Ermeni Patrikhanesi)

**MAP M6** ■ **Sevgi Sok 6, Kumkapı**

The Armenians came in numbers to Istanbul in

**Detail, Fatih Mosque**

1461, invited by Sultan Mehmet the Conqueror to help rebuild the city after its capture in 1453. Opposite the attractive patriarchate building, the Church of the Holy Mother of God (Surp Asdvadzadzin) serves as the main church for the now sadly dwindling Armenian community.

### 8 Church of St Mary of the Mongols (Kanlı Kilise)

Princess Maria, illegitimate daughter of Byzantine Emperor Michael VIII Palaeologos, married Khan Abaqa of the Mongols. On his death in 1282, she founded a convent and this church – Istanbul's only Greek Orthodox church to have been granted immunity from conversion to a mosque by Mehmet the Conqueror (see p78).

### 9 Christ Church

Consecrated in 1868 as the Crimean Memorial Church, this fine Gothic Revival building was renovated and renamed in the 1990s. It is the largest Protestant church in Istanbul (see p86).

### 10 Church of St Anthony of Padua (Sent Antuan Kilisesi)

The Church of St Anthony of Padua is Istanbul's largest Roman Catholic church. Built in 1906–12, it is home to a small community of Franciscan monks (see p86).

**Neo-Gothic façade of the Church of St Anthony of Padua, Beyoğlu**

**TOP 10 TIPS ON ISLAMIC ETIQUETTE**

**Women in headscarves**

**1 Shoes**
Remove your shoes before entering a mosque or a Turkish home.

**2 Men and Women**
A man should not touch a woman (other than family), even to shake hands, unless the woman proffers her hand or cheek first.

**3 Left Hand**
In some Islamic countries one should avoid eating or passing food with the left hand; in Turkey this is not observed.

**4 Pork and Alcohol**
Although many people in Turkey do drink alcohol, you should never offer alcohol or pork to a Muslim – and do not consume any yourself if unsure of your companions' views.

**5 Family Rooms**
Some restaurants and cafés have separate family rooms (aile salonu) into which women will automatically be conducted. Men may only sit there with their families.

**6 Dress**
Dress modestly – no bare knees, shoulders or midriffs (for either sex).

**7 Covering the Head**
It is essential for women to cover their heads when entering a mosque.

**8 Ramazan (Ramadan)**
Avoid eating and drinking in public during daylight hours in the month-long fast of Ramazan.

**9 Sightseeing**
Don't go sightseeing in mosques at prayer times (particularly around midday on Fridays).

**10 Joking about Islam**
Don't joke about Islam or criticize anything related to it.

# 🔟 **Museums and Galleries**

**Bright exterior of the Istanbul Modern**

## 1 Istanbul Modern

For centuries, Turkish art was better known for tradition rather than innovation, but contemporary Turkish artists are exploring new avenues. Set in a beautifully converted Bosphorus warehouse, Istanbul Modern is an ideal platform for showcasing art from the 19th to the 21st centuries (see p91).

## 2 Topkapı Palace
(Topkapı Sarayı)

The buildings are spectacular, some of the collections are even more so – from the sea of Chinese porcelain in the kitchens to the Treasury, with its ostentatious display of jewellery, carved ivory and great rocks of emerald. Religious treasures include hair from the Prophet's beard (see pp12–15).

**Ceramic pot at the Pera Museum in Beyoğlu**

## 3 Archaeological Museum
(Arkeoloji Müzesi)

Don't miss the late 4th-century-AD marble tomb of Abdalonymus of Sidon, known as the "Alexander Sarcophagus". Its high-relief carving depicts Alexander the Great defeating the Persians at the Battle of Issus in 333 BC (see pp20–21).

## 4 Military Museum
(Askeri Müze)

Among the many fascinating exhibits at this museum are curved daggers (cembiyes) carried by 15th-century Ottoman foot soldiers, and the vast imperial tents used by sultans during their military campaigns. The Mehter Band, founded in the 14th century, plays Ottoman military music daily at 3pm (see p84).

## 5 Pera Museum
(Pera Müzesi)

The Pera is a privately run museum with an intriguing mix of fine art, modern exhibitions and ancient weights and measures (see p85).

## 6 Sakıp Sabancı Museum
(Sakıp Sabancı Müzesi)

Known locally as the "Horse Mansion", this lovely museum houses the collection of the late Turkish business tycoon Sakıp Sabancı. The displays encompass 500 years of Ottoman calligraphy, and Ottoman and Turkish painting of the 19th and 20th centuries. Major touring art exhibitions are also hosted here (see p93).

## 7 Museum of Turkish and Islamic Arts
(Türk ve İslam Eserleri Müzesi)

This wonderful collection, in the 16th-century palace of İbrahim Paşa, spans 1,300 years of the finest works of Turkish and Islamic art. Among the exhibits are splendid Turkish carpets, calligraphy and ethnographic items *(see p61)*.

## 8 Rahmi Koç Museum
(Rahmi Koç Müzesi)

An Ottoman foundry and nearby shipyard on the Golden Horn are the perfect setting for this world-class collection of all things mechanical, from vintage cars to model planes – and even a submarine *(see pp76-77)*.

## 9 Sadberk Hanım Museum
(Sadberk Hanım Müzesi)

Two lovingly restored Bosphorus mansions house an inspiring collection of ancient Anatolian artifacts, Ottoman costumes and ceramics *(see p93)*.

**Sadberk Hanım Museum, on the banks of the Bosphorus**

## 10 Naval Museum
(Deniz Müzesi)

For centuries, the Ottoman navy ruled the seas, and its achievements are celebrated in this marvellous museum. Among the exhibits are figureheads and engravings, but the flamboyantly decorated royal barges are the highlight of any visit *(see p91)*.

---

**TOP 10 LESSER-KNOWN MUSEUMS**

SALT Beyoğlu

**1 Ottoman Bank Museum**
MAP F3 ▪ Bankalar Cad 11, Galata ▪ (0212) 334 22 00
Delve into the intriguing vaults of a bank designed by Vallaury in 1890.

**2 Mevlevi Monastery**
Whirling dervishes are the main draw in this monastery-turned-museum *(see p84)*.

**3 SALT Beyoğlu**
Gallery complex housed in a beautifully restored 19th century apartment block on busy Istiklal Caddesi *(see p54)*.

**4 Railway Museum, Sirkeci Station**
The *Orient Express* silver service is the star among 300 exhibits *(see p62)*.

**5 SAV Automobile Museum**
Inspect some of the best motor transport from the last century, from Rolls-Royce to Ferrari *(see p94)*.

**6 Aşiyan Museum**
A Bosphorus mansion pays homage to 20th-century poets and thinkers *(see p92)*.

**7 Museum of the History of Science and Technology in Islam**
MAP G4 ▪ Has Ahirlar Binası, Gülhane Parkı ▪ (0212) 528 80 65
See displays of historical tools from astronomy and medicine, to war.

**8 Florence Nightingale Museum**
The museum includes the nurse's private quarters and surgery room used during the Crimean War *(see p97)*.

**9 Arter Gallery**
MAP J5 ▪ İstiklal Cad 211 ▪ (0212) 243 37 67
The gallery hosts temporary exhibitions by internationally acclaimed artists.

**10 Atatürk Museum**
MAP T3 ▪ Halaskargazi Cad, Şişli ▪ (0212) 240 63 19
This suburban house is now a memorial museum to the great man.

# 🔟 Off the Beaten Track

### ① Safa Meyhanesi

**MAP A6** ■ İlyasbey
**Cad 121, Yedikule** ■ **(0212) 585 55 94**

Arguably the city's most atmospheric
*meyhane* (tavern), located in the historic Yedikule quarter, a short stroll
from the fortress of the same name.
The decor hasn't changed since the
1940s, with vintage *rakı* (aniseed
spirit) posters adorning the walls,
high ceilings and wooden floors.
Drink *rakı*, eat *meze* and fish and
be merry.

**Jewish Museum**

### ② Jewish Museum

**MAP F2** ■ Neve Shalom
Synagogue, Büyük Hendek Cad 61,
Karaköy ■ **(0212) 244 15 76**
■ Open 10am–4pm Mon–Thu, 10am–
2pm Fri & Sun ■ Adm charge
■ www.muze500.com

This interesting little museum is
housed in the Nev Shalom synagogue,
near the Galata Tower. The museum
tells the story of the Jews who
were offered sanctuary in Istanbul
following their expulsion from
Spain in the late 15th century.

### ③ Zoodochus Pege
(Balıklı Kilise)

**MAP A6** ■ Seyit Nizam Cad 3,
Silivrikapı ■ **(0212) 582 30 81**
■ Open 8.30am–4:30pm daily

This beautiful 19th-century Greek
Orthodox church is set in lush
green Christian and Muslim
cemeteries. In a basement shrine,
holy carp swim gracefully in the
crystal-clear spring waters.

### ④ Depo

**MAP G2** ■ Koltukçular
Çıkmaz, Beyoğlu ■ **(0212) 292
39 56** ■ Open 11am–7pm Tue–
Sun ■ www.depoistanbul.net

Housed in a former tobacco
warehouse, this hip but socially
conscious gallery has an ever-
changing series of exhibitions.
Many of the shows focus on
more offbeat subjects, such as
the plight of Turkey's Christian
minorities, political protests and
the like. There are also regular
documentary screenings.

### 5 Column of Marcian
(Kıztaşı)

**MAP C4** ■ Junction of Kıztaşı Cad with Dolap Sokak, Aksaray

Less tall but more impressive than the better-known Çemberlitaş (Column of Constantine), this 5th-century granite column still has an ornately carved Corinthian capital adorned with eagles and a plinth carved with Nike, goddess of victory.

### 6 Mihrimah Mosque
(Mihrimah Cami)

**MAP J3** ■ Sulukule Cad, Edirnekapı ■ Open dawn–dusk daily

A masterpiece of the Ottoman architect Sinan and dedicated to the beautiful Mihrimah, daughter of Sultan Süleyman the Magnificent, this delightful mosque stands dramatically atop the old city's highest hill. Its elegant interior is flooded with light from attractive stained-glass windows.

**Ornate dome, Mihrimah Mosque**

### 7 Vefa Bozacısı

**MAP E4** ■ Vefa Cad 66, Fatih ■ 0212 519 49 22 ■ www.vefa.com.tr ■ Open 7am–midnight daily

Even if you don't fancy drinking the fermented millet drink *(boza)* for which this charming place is known, it's worth coming for the late-19th-century interior, with its cut glass, dark wood and blue-and-white İznik tiles. The *boza* is made out back.

### 8 Istanbul Municipality Building

**MAP D4** ■ Sehzadebaşı Cad, Fatih ■ (0212) 512 55 00

Built in 1953, this huge, rectangular building's grid-like façade brought international, modern architecture into the heart of the old city, apposite when you consider that Le Corbusier was influenced by Ottoman architecture following a visit to the city in 1911.

### 9 Edirnekapı Pigeon Fanciers' Market
(Güvercin Pazarı)

**MAP J1**

Every Saturday and Sunday, pigeon fanciers from across the city come to buy and sell tumbling pigeons at this fascinating bazaar in the shadow of the Byzantine Palace of the Porphyrogenitus *(see p78)*. Drink a refreshing glass of tea with the old-timers in the teahouse opposite and soak up the atmosphere.

### 10 Emirgan Park

Istanbul's most beautiful park is located by the Bosphorus, just above the second suspension bridge. Dotted with *kösks*, little wooden pavilions resembling Swiss chalets, it has a small lake and some children's play equipment. The park is awash with blooms during April's Tulip Festival *(see p56)* and provides a pleasant retreat from the city *(see p94)*.

**Resplendent Emirgan Park during the Tulip Festival**

# 🔟 Culinary Highlights

### 1 Meze

Most Turkish meals begin with *meze* – collections of small starters. The range of *meze* is vast, and you can easily eat enough for a whole meal. Cold options range from *haydari* (yoghurt with mint and garlic) to *midye pilakisi* (mussels cooked in olive oil) or *çerkez tavuğu* (cold chicken in walnut and bread sauce). Hot options may include chicken liver kebabs, calamari, grilled cheese, or something more adventurous such as *koç yumurtası* (fried sheep's testicles).

### 2 İmam Bayıldı ("The Imam Fainted")

This strangely named dish of aubergine stuffed with tomatoes and onions is a Turkish classic – the Imam in question supposedly found it so delicious that he passed out in ecstasy. Aubergine is a fundamental ingredient of Turkish cuisine; it is said that Ottoman court chefs could prepare it in 150 ways.

*İmam Bayıldı*

### 3 Dolma

The word *dolma* means "filled up", and is used to describe any stuffed food, from walnuts to peppers, beef tomatoes or aubergine.

The most common version, eaten cold, is vine leaves stuffed with rice, onion, nuts and herbs.

### 4 Kebabs and Köfte

Turkey's most famous culinary export is the kebab – called *kebap* in Turkish. *Döner kebap* is wafer-thin slices of roast meat (usually lamb) carved from a spit; the *şiş kebap* is cubed lamb or chicken grilled on a skewer. *Köfte* is minced meat cooked as meatballs or flattened onto a skewer and grilled as an *ızgara kebap*.

### 5 Çoban Salatası ("Shepherd's Salad")

This salad combines tomato, cucumber, chopped pepper, lettuce, coriander, celery, lemon juice and olive oil in a light, healthy, colourful and refreshing dish. Turkish tomatoes are among the finest in the world.

### 6 Seafood

Istanbul's proximity to the sea means that *taze balık* (fresh fish) is very popular with locals. The catch of the day is often grilled and served with rice or chips and salad. Shellfish and calamari are served as *meze*. A delicious Black Sea dish is *hamsi pilavı* (fresh anchovies and rice).

**Stuffed vine leaves or *dolma***

**7 Stews** (Güveç)
Often served in traditional *lokanta* restaurants (see p110) and generally popular in winter, hearty stews are mostly made with lamb, tomatoes and onions.

**8 Börek**
These savoury pastries are served either as part of a *meze* tray or on their own as fast food. They can be flat or rolled, and are filled with cheese and parsley, spinach or meat. They make an excellent light snack.

**Turkish pastries**

**9 Pastries**
Sweet pastries are sold in dedicated shops and by street vendors; tourist restaurants will offer them as dessert. The most famous is baklava (flaky pastry drenched in syrup), but there are many variations with honey, syrups, marzipan, almonds and pistachios. All are heaven to eat and calorie hell.

**10 Tea and Coffee**
The lifeblood of Turkey, both *çay* (tea) and *kahve* (coffee) are drunk black, strong and sweet, in small quantities. Tea is served all day and on all occasions. You can ask for it weaker (*açık*) and without sugar. Coffee is drunk less frequently; it is more expensive than tea, and is served with a glass of water. All instant coffee is known as Nescafé.

**Traditional black tea with lemon**

---

**TOP 10 CULINARY SPECIALITIES**

*Gözleme*

**1 Elastic Ice Cream**
*Maraş dondurması* uses wild orchid tubers as a thickening agent. The ice cream is able to stretch into a "rope" 60 cm (2 ft) long!

**2 İşkembe Çorbası** (Tripe Soup)
This local delicacy is said to be very good for hangovers.

**3 Kanlıca Yoghurt**
Firm and creamy, the yoghurt from Kanlıca is the country's finest.

**4 Lokum** (Turkish Delight)
MAP Q2 ▪ Hamidiye Cad 81, Bahçekapı ▪ (0212) 522 85 43
Turkish delight was invented by an Istanbul sweetmaker (see p38). It's now sold everywhere and in many flavours. The original shop on Hamidiye Caddesi is still open.

**5 Simit**
A *simit* is a round sesame bread, much like a New York pretzel.

**6 Gözleme**
A *gözleme* is a large rolled pancake with savoury stuffing.

**7 Mantı**
These pasta packets are stuffed with minced lamb and served in a thin garlic sauce.

**8 Aşure** (Noah's Pudding)
As the story goes, this celebratory pudding was first made by Mrs Noah, from whatever scraps remained on the Ark at the end of the flood.

**9 Elma Çayı** (Apple Tea)
You may be offered this as an alternative to ordinary tea when visiting carpet shops.

**10 Rakı**
A clear spirit, *rakı* is usually an aniseed-based liquor similar to Greek *ouzo* that is drunk after being diluted with water.

# 🔟 Restaurants

**Alfresco dining at Asitane**

### 1 Asitane

The complex flavours of Ottoman court cuisine are resurrected (based on extensive research) at Asitane. Hundreds of years later, almond soup, melon stuffed with minced lamb and goose kebabs are still fit for a sultan (see p79).

### 2 İmroz

MAP K4 ▪ Nevizade Sokak 24, Beyoğlu ▪ (0212) 249 90 73 ▪ ₺

Established in 1941, this is one of the liveliest, best-value *meyhanes* (taverns) on Nevizade Sokak. Go for the fixed-price menu.

### 3 Yeni Lokanta

MAP J6 ▪ Kumbaracı Yokuşu 66, Beyoğlu ▪ (0212) 292 25 50 ▪ ₺₺₺

One of the few Beyoğlu restaurants to attract well-heeled Istanbulites in from the suburbs, this stylish place concentrates on good, solid Turkish dishes with a few modern twists. Book well in advance.

### 4 Seasons Restaurant

The Seasons is the restaurant of the Four Seasons Hotel, which was once an Ottoman prison. Glass rather than thick

walls now encloses its pretty courtyard garden. The modern Mediterranean food is imaginative and delicious, and the service is attentive (see p67).

### 5 Feriye Lokantası

Situated in a 19th-century police station on the Bosphorus shore, this fashionable restaurant is taking a fresh look at Turkish cuisine, combining traditional recipes with European flair in one of the most exciting culinary experiences in the city (see p95).

### 6 Akdeniz Hatay Sofrası

MAP A6 ▪ Ahmediye Cad 44/A, Aksaray ▪ (0212) 444 7 247 ▪ ₺

**Akdeniz Hatay Sofrası**

This bustling place serves up the best southeast Turkish food in the city. The tangy *meze* are excellent, the rice-stuffed chicken roasted in a salt crust and metre-long kebabs a delight.

### 7 Mikla

MAP J5 ▪ The Marmara Pera, Meşrutiyet Cad 15, Beyoğlu ▪ (0212) 293 56 56 ▪ ₺₺

Reserve a terrace table at the Marmara Pera Hotel's stylish rooftop restaurant for the perfect view of the Golden Horn – and across the city, 17 floors below. The Mediterranean cuisine has Turkish and Nordic touches. The decor is elegant – there's even a swimming pool by the bar. Grab a cocktail and sink into one of the soft sofas.

**Seasons Restaurant**

The terrace at 360

**⑧ 360**

Rub shoulders with the swanky young set of Istanbul on 360's superb terrace bar, taking your time to drink in the stunning views of both the Bosphorus and the Golden Horn, then withdraw to the spacious, well-lit interior to sample such eclectic delights as samphire and soya sprouts, Vietnamese beef tartare, polenta-crusted calamari, seafood risotto, lamb loin confit, Margarita sorbet and pistachio baklava *(see p88)*.

**⑨ Balıkçı Sabahattin**

A truly traditional Turkish experience, this wonderful fish restaurant (open since 1927) is situated in an old house with antique carpets and copper pots. There's also an outdoor terrace with lively Gypsy violinists. The food is excellent, although there is no menu – you choose from a wide range of *meze* and the catch of the day *(see p67)*.

**⑩ Giritli**

Cretan dishes such as *ceviche*-style sea bass and cracked green olives cured in brine transport diners to their own little Greek island for the night. The fixed-price menu includes unlimited glasses of wine, a selection of *meze* and perfectly prepared fish. The restored historic house location and pretty restaurant garden are a bonus *(see p67)*.

---

### TOP 10 ENTERTAINMENT VENUES

**1 Al Jamal**
Offers a luxurious evening of top-notch food and belly dancing *(see p88)*.

**2 Hodja Pasha Cultural Centre**
MAP T4 ▪ Hoca Paşa Hamam Sok 3, Sirkeci ▪ (0212) 511 46 26
▪ www.hodjapasha.com
This Ottoman period bathhouse is the venue for folk and Whirling dervish performances.

**3 Babylon**
One of the best sound systems in town to celebrate rock, world music and other acts *(see p88)*.

**4 Cemal Reşit Rey Concert Hall**
MAP B4 ▪ Darülbedayı Cad 1, Harbiye ▪ (0212) 232 98 30
▪ www.crrkonsersalonu.org
Daily concerts include Western and Turkish classical, and world music.

**5 Aksanat (Akbank) Cultural Centre**
MAP L4 ▪ İstiklal Cad 8 ▪ (0212) 252 35 00 ▪ www.akbanksanat.com
This arts centre offers music and theatre.

**6 Zorlu Centre**
A performing arts centre, which hosts classical and pop concerts *(see p53)*.

**7 Ortaköy**
The Bosphorus suburb of Ortaköy is home to a string of popular nightclubs including Anjelique, Reina and Blackk.

**8 Nardis Jazz Club**
Live jazz performed in an intimate setting *(see p88)*.

**9 Salon İKSV**
Istanbul's top arts organization hosts great classical and jazz concerts, plus theatre and film *(see p88)*.

**10 Süreyya Opera House**
MAP U4 ▪ Bahariye Cad 29, Kadıköy
▪ (0216) 346 15 31
This Art-Deco-inspired 1920s theatre hosts opera and ballet.

*Single City play at Salon İKSV*

*For a key to restaurant price ranges see p67*

# Shops and Markets

### 1 Grand Bazaar
(Kapalı Çarşı)

One of the oldest, biggest and most exciting shopping malls in the world, the Grand Bazaar was set up to trade silk, spices and gold in the 15th century – and still sells all three, alongside jazzy glass lampshades, leather jackets and, of course, Turkish carpets *(see pp22–3)*.

**Grand Bazaar**

### 2 Egyptian Bazaar
(Mısır Çarşısı)

Also known as the Spice Bazaar, this is the best place in town to buy little presents, with a sea of spice stalls, piles of Turkish delight and plenty of cheap and cheerful souvenirs *(see pp70-71)*.

### 3 Çarşamba Street Market
(Çarşamba Pazarı)

MAP C3

So famous is this lively street market that the entire district is named Çarşamba (Wednesday) after the day of the week it is held. Many stalls are stacked with fruit, vegetables, cheeses, spices, dried fruit and nuts. Others concentrate on cheap clothing, while more traditional items include thin wooden rolling pins used to make flat breads, and brass coffee grinders. The sprawling market stalls occupy

several streets to the north and west of Fatih Mosque where the area is devoutly Muslim.

### 4 İstiklal Caddesi

The city's main modern shopping street, İstiklal is packed day and night throughout the week. If you need a break from hunting for bargain designer clothes (in İş Merkezi) or the perfect glass teacups (in Paşabahçe), there are plenty of cafés to choose from *(see p86)*.

### 5 Nişantaşı
MAP C4

Nişantaşı and neighbouring Teşvikiye are where local fashionistas spend their money on international brands, including Versace and Dior. It is perhaps less exciting for those who can get the same thing at home.

### 6 Arasta Bazaar
(Arasta Çarşısı)

This small, upmarket bazaar offers the best souvenir shopping in Sultanahmet. Originally built to provide money for the upkeep of the Blue Mosque, it sells good-quality carpets, jewellery and handicrafts in a relatively calm environment, conveniently close to many major sights and hotels *(see p64 & p114)*.

**Second-Hand Book Bazaar**

### 7 Second-Hand Book Bazaar (Sahaflar Çarşısı)

The Second-Hand Book Bazaar started out selling scraps of parchment with Koranic text. Today, it mainly stocks textbooks and coffee-table books about Turkey *(see p72)*.

## ⑧ Zorlu Centre

MAP C4 ■ Koru Sokak, Zincirlikuyu ■ (0850) 222 67 76 ■ www.zorlucenter.com

Designed by Turkey's leading architecture practice, Tabanlioğlu, this state-of-the-art mall in a suburb overlooking the Bosphorus Bridge is worth seeing in its own right. It contains the PSM performance hall, a host of trendy shops and a high-tech cinema, as well as Istanbul Raffles Hotel.

**The upmarket shopping mall, Kanyon**

## ⑨ Kanyon, Levent

MAP U3

Join the city's most stylish shoppers at Kanyon, Istanbul's most architecturally distinctive shopping mall.

## ⑩ Çukurcuma, Galatasaray

Many travellers fall in love with this charming old quarter of Beyoğlu, with its eclectic range of antiques and second-hand dealers, whose wares flow out onto the streets around Turnacıbaşı Sokağı. Great for a morning's browsing *(see p87)*.

**Çukurcuma antique shop**

---

### TOP 10 THINGS TO BUY

**Traditional glass bead jewellery**

**1 Carpets**
Carpets are the true glory of Turkish art – and you can have one on your own hall floor.

**2 Jewellery**
Precious metals are sold by weight, with a mark-up for workmanship. There are plenty of options, including designing your own jewellery.

**3 Leather**
Jackets, bags, wallets and belts are great value and come in all styles, colours and qualities. Again, have your ideas custom-designed if you have enough time.

**4 Clothes**
Shop around and you can find good-quality clothes and great design at reasonable prices.

**5 Textiles**
Both cottons and silks are made here, and are reasonably priced. Silk scarves are a great-value present.

**6 Spices**
Great heaps of coloured spices are hard to resist. If you buy saffron, check it's the real thing – there's a cheaper alternative (safflower) on sale.

**7 Historic Reproductions**
Reproduction Ottoman miniatures are easy to carry and look great back at home.

**8 Souvenirs**
Shop for hand-woven towels and items hand-made from felt.

**9 Blue Beads**
The ubiquitous blue bead is actually a charm to ward off the "evil eye"; believe that or not, they make attractive gifts.

**10 Food**
Turkish delight, almonds and hazelnuts, pomegranate molasses and all sorts of other comestibles make great presents.

# 🔟 Istanbul for Free

### 1 Misir Apartment
MAP J5
■ Istiklal Cad 163, Beyoğlu

This stylish Art Nouveau apartment block is home to a number of small but well-regarded art galleries, including Galeri Zilberman and Galerist. It's also worth heading up to the chic rooftop bar-restaurant, 360 *(see p51)*. Here, you can enjoy a free panorama of Istanbul or treat yourself to a pricey drink.

### 2 Ottoman Mosques
One of Istanbul's greatest glories is its stunning array of domed Ottoman-era mosques, each flanked by one or more slender minarets. Many of the mosques have delightful interiors encrusted with pretty İznik tiles; all have that indefinable air of tranquillity and sanctity.

### 3 Park Life
With a population of at least 14 million, Istanbul can seem an incredibly congested city. Join the locals and escape to one of the city's green and historic parks. The best of these are Emirgan *(see p94)*, Yıldız on the Bosphorus and Gülhane in the old city.

**Down time in Gülhane Park**

**Visual presentation, SALT Beyoğlu**

### 4 SALT Beyoğlu
MAP J5 ■ İstiklal Cad 163, Beyoğlu ■ (0212) 377 42 00 ■ www.saltonline.org

This non-profitmaking gallery opened in a grand old 19th-century apartment block on bustling İstiklal Caddesi in 2011, and is now one of the city's premier exhibition spaces. There's also a café, bookshop, archive and library, and roof terrace.

### 5 Walking the Theodosian Walls
These 5th-century triple defences saved Constantinople from Attila the Hun and many others for over 1,000 years. They have survived remarkably well, and walking their 6-km (4-mile) length from the Sea of Marmara north to the Golden Horn is a series of fascinating steps back into the past *(see p77)*.

### 6 Churches
Many Byzantine churches were turned into mosques during the Ottoman era, but the city retained a substantial Christian community until after World War I. Many are still in use and give a glimpse into the lives of a dwindling community. Try the 19th-century St Stephen of the Bulgars or the nearby Greek Orthodox Church of St George *(see p78)*.

### 7 Ottoman Bank Museum
MAP F3 ■ Bankalar Cad 11, Karaköy ■ (0212) 334 22 00 ■ www.saltonline.org

A trip to the immaculately preserved vaults of an iconic late Ottoman bank really brings to life what this most cosmopolitan of neighbourhoods was like, with its Muslim Turks, Jews, Christian Armenians and Greeks. Pop upstairs to see a free exhibition in SALT Galata, sister branch to SALT Beyoğlu.

### 8 Research Centre for Anatolian Civilizations

**MAP J5 ■ Merkez Han, İstiklal Cad 181, Beyoğlu ■ (0212) 393 60 00 ■ www.rcac.ku.edu.tr/en**

For well-presented exhibitions of an archaeological, historical or cultural nature, this ground-floor display space is just great. The centre is part of Koç University and has a well-stocked specialist library upstairs.

### 9 Sultan Sarnıç

**MAP D2 ■ Yavuz Selim Cad, Fatih ■ (0212) 521 07 20**

This Byzantine cistern is smaller and less conveniently located, but is just as stunning as the famous Basilica Cistern *(see p63)*, with floodlit columns carved with Christian crosses and surmounted by ornate capitals. The Sultan Sarnıç cistern is usually open to visitors daily from 9am until early evening unless there is a function on.

**Karaköy Fish Market**

### 10 Karaköy Fish Market

**MAP F3**

Just west of the Galata Bridge in Karaköy is a small but authentic fish market; look out for the *hamsi* (anchovies) piled up in season. Walk west along the scruffy waterfront towards the Haliç metro bridge and admire the ferry-filled waters of the Golden Horn backed by the old city's skyline of mosques and minarets.

**TOP 10 MONEY-SAVING TIPS**

**Street food vendors**

**1 Discounts**
For discounts on Istanbul's top sights, get a Museum Pass.
**www.muzekart.com/en**

**2 Public Transport**
The Istanbulkart saves up to 25 per cent per journey on public transport.
**www.istanbulkart.iett.gov.tr/en**

**3 Entertainment**
Numerous buskers and street entertainers perform on Beyoğlu's İstiklal Caddesi.

**4 Alcohol**
Restaurants that serve alcohol with meals are always more expensive.

**5 Art Galleries**
There are many free art galleries around İstiklal Caddesi, and street art in bohemian Galata.

**6 Street Food**
Street vendors sell cheap snacks, such as bagel-like *simits*, rice and chickpeas and *kokoreç* (stuffed lamb intestines).

**7 Clothing**
For cheap clothes, try Beyoğlu İş Merkezi at İstiklal Cad 331, or Terkoz Çıkmaz İş Merkezi, off İstiklal Caddesi.

**8 Bazaar**
The streets surrounding the historic Spice Bazaar are better value than the market itself.

**9 Ferries**
Ferries up the Golden Horn or the Princes' Islands are as enjoyable, but cheaper, than the Bosphorus Cruise.

**10 Nightlife**
For a lively night at a *meyhane* (tavern), it is cheaper to get the all-inclusive deal with unlimited drinks.

# TOP 10 Festivals and Events

**Colourful display at Istanbul's Tulip Festival**

### 1 Tulip Festival
**Apr ■ Parks across the city**

Turkey's national flower is the tulip (*lale*). The tulip motif appeared endlessly on İznik tiles and today can be seen on Turkish Airlines aircraft. Each April millions of bulbs bloom across the city, with a competition to judge the best 100. Roadside verges become a riot of colour, but the flowers are best viewed in parks such as Emirgan and Gülhane.

**International Istanbul Film Festival**

### 2 International Istanbul Film Festival
**Apr ■ Various venues ■ (0212) 334 07 00 ■ www.iksv.org**

Since its inception in 1982, this festival has screened over 3,000 films from 76 countries. A highlight of the festival is the Award for Lifetime Achievement, instituted in 1996 – winners include French stars Alain Delon and Jeanne Moreau. Most screenings are held in cinemas around İstiklal Caddesi.

### 3 One Love Festival
**Jul ■ Call to check venue ■ (0212) 334 01 00 ■ www.pozitif.info**

This two-day midsummer extravaganza combines top international acts like Morrissey, Black Eyed Peas and Manu Chao with Turkish rock and dance bands.

### 4 International Istanbul Music and Dance Festival
**Jun ■ Various venues ■ (0212) 334 07 00 ■ www.iksv.org**

An impressive array of soloists, ensembles and orchestras has graced the stages of this prestigious festival since it was established in 1973. Mozart's opera *The Abduction from the Seraglio* is staged each year in Topkapı Palace.

### 5 International Asia-to-Europe Swimming, Rowing and Sailing Competitions
**Jul ■ (0212) 560 07 07 ■ www.bogazici.cc**

Competitors in this trio of events cross the Bosphorus from a variety of starting points: Kanlıca for swimmers, Arnavutköy for rowers and Kandilli for yachtsmen. All three races end at Kuruçeşme. Other events include water-skiing, jet-skiing and underwater-swimming displays.

### ⑥ Feast of Sacrifice
(Kurban Bayramı)
**Four days, dates vary**

Also known as Eid-ul-Adha, the Feast of Sacrifice commemorates the Koranic version of Abraham's sacrifice. It falls two months and ten days after the end of Ramazan (Ramadan). Muslims celebrate by slaughtering a sheep on the morning of the first day of the festival. Friends and family are invited to a lavish meal, but much of the meat goes to charity. Note that this is Turkey's major annual public holiday – nearly everything closes, and public transport is seriously stretched.

### ⑦ International Istanbul Jazz Festival
**Jul ▪ Various venues ▪ (0212) 334 07 00 ▪ www.iksv.org**

The Jazz Festival's origins lie in a concert by Chick Corea and Steve Kujala at the 1984 Istanbul Music Festival. It was established as an independent event in 1994. The musical range is broad, and you are as likely to encounter Björk or Elvis Costello as you are Brad Mehldau. The choice of venues is eclectic, with traditional clubs, outdoor stages and even a boat cruising on the Bosphorus.

### ⑧ Istanbul Eurasia Marathon
**Nov ▪ Call ahead for tickets ▪ (0212) 453 30 00 ▪ www.istanbulmarathon.org**

Every November, athletes have the chance to take part in the world's only transcontinental marathon with

**Istanbul Eurasia Marathon**

the Bosphorus Bridge closed for part of the day to allow those taking part to cross from Europe to Asia.

### ⑨ Sugar Festival
(Şeker Ramazan Bayramı)
**Three days, dates vary**

The Sugar Festival marks the end of the fasting month of Ramazan. People hand out sweets, visit relatives and enjoy cultural events – and Istanbul's bars and clubs are busy again. Many take advantage of the holiday period and head out of the city for a few days to escape the hustle and bustle.

### ⑩ International Istanbul Fine Arts Biennial
**Sep–Nov, every other year (odd numbers) ▪ Various venues ▪ (0212) 334 07 00 ▪ www.iksv.org**

Istanbul's Biennial showcases contemporary visual arts from Turkey and around the globe. Each festival is directed by a curator of a different nationality, who chooses a theme and arranges the programme of exhibitions, conferences and workshops.

**Henning Schmeidt Ensemble at the International Istanbul Jazz Festival**

# Istanbul
# Area by Area

Sunset views across the city to
Galata Tower from Topkapı Palace

# 🔟 Sultanahmet and the Old City

**Egyptian Obelisk, Hippodrome**

Many of the city's greatest sights are to be found in this historic area, which was in turn the centre of Byzantium, Constantinople and Ottoman Istanbul. Archaeologists have dated settlements in this strategic spot at the entrance to the Golden Horn to the 6th millennium BC, but recorded history begins around 667 BC, when Greek colonist Byzas founded Byzantion on Seraglio Point (now home to the Topkapı Palace). After his arrival in AD 324, Constantine transformed this port into the dazzling jewel of Constantinople, a new capital for the Roman Empire. By 1453, when the Ottomans seized power, the city was run-down and ruinous, and the new rulers stamped their authority – both religious and secular – on its buildings.

**1 Haghia Sophia** (Ayasofya)

Consecrated by Justinian in 537, the "Church of Holy Wisdom" is an enduring tribute to the skill of its architects, Anthemius of Tralles and Isidore of Miletus, who created a monument that has withstood wars and earthquakes. The scale of its vast central dome was not surpassed until the construction of St Peter's in Rome, 1,000 years later *(see pp16–17)*.

**2 Hippodrome** (At Meydanı)
MAP Q5

Now a peaceful park, the Hippodrome was the Byzantine chariot racetrack – a stadium capable of holding 100,000 people. Laid out in the 3rd century AD by Emperor Septimius Severus, it was enlarged and connected to the adjacent Great Palace by Constantine. There are three great monuments in the Hippodrome: the Egyptian Obelisk, the Obelisk of Theodosius (Dikilitaş), of c.1500 BC, which Theodosius transported from Luxor; the Serpentine Column (Yılanlı Sütun) from the Temple of Apollo at Delphi in Greece, made in 479 BC; and the Column

of Constantine VII Porphryogenitus (Ormetaş), which is of unknown date and was named after the emperor who had it restored in the 10th century. The stadium once held four great bronze horses, but these were looted by the Crusaders in 1204 and now grace St Mark's Cathedral in Venice.

**3 Blue Mosque** (Sultanahmet Camii)

Begun in 1609, Sultan Ahmet I's mosque was built opposite Haghia Sophia and directly on top of Constantine's Great Palace to stress the supremacy of Islam and the Ottoman Empire over Christian Byzantium *(see pp18–19)*.

**The Blue Mosque**

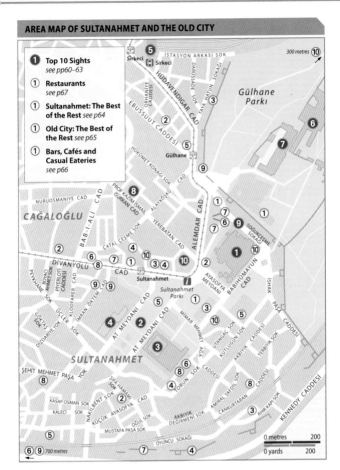

## AREA MAP OF SULTANAHMET AND THE OLD CITY

1 **Top 10 Sights**
*see pp60–63*

1 **Restaurants**
*see p67*

1 **Sultanahmet: The Best of the Rest** *see p64*

1 **Old City: The Best of the Rest** *see p65*

1 **Bars, Cafés and Casual Eateries**
*see p66*

4 **Museum of Turkish and Islamic Arts**
(Türk ve İslam Eserleri Müzesi)
MAP Q5 ▪ At Meydanı Cad 46 ▪
(0212) 518 18 05 ▪ Open daily Apr–
Oct: 9am–7pm; Nov–Mar: 9am–5pm
▪ Adm charge ▪ www.tiem.gov.tr

This museum is housed in the palace built by İbrahim Paşa (c.1493–1536), Grand Vizier to Süleyman the Magnificent. It contains a collection of more than 40,000 artifacts dating from the 7th century to the present, with exhibits of fine art, crafts and Turkish domestic life in its evolution from nomad's tent to modern home.

**Museum of Turkish and Islamic Arts**

**Detail, Sirkeci Station**

### 5 Sirkeci Station
(Sirkeci Garı)

MAP R2 ▪ İstasyon Arkasi Sok ▪ (0212) 520 65 75 ▪ Museum open 9am–5pm Tue–Sat

Officially opened in November 1890, the glamorous eastern terminus for the *Orient Express* service was built by German architect August Jasmund in an eclectic style drawing together elements of Istanbul's varied architectural traditions. The station also houses a railway museum *(see p45)* and a modest restaurant. Since the opening of the Marmaray line in 2013 this grand old station is no longer the terminus for trains from Europe, but a mere stop on the metro – albeit the last one before the continent-linking Bosphorus Tunnel.

### 6 Topkapı Palace
(Topkapı Sarayı)

The great palace of the Ottoman Empire was both the residence and the centre of government of the early sultans. The whole complex can take a full day to explore; highlights include the Harem and the Treasury *(see pp12–13)*.

### 7 Archaeological Museum
(Arkeoloji Müzesi)

This is one of the world's great historical museums. It has three principal sections: the Museum of the Ancient Orient, which contains, among other things, the city gates of Babylon; the Tiled Kiosk, with a superb display of ceramics; and the main museum, where royal sarcophagi found at Sidon in Lebanon are star exhibits *(see pp20–21)*.

### 8 Cağaloğlu Baths
(Cağaloğlu Hamamı)

MAP Q3 ▪ Prof Kazım İsmail Gürkan Cad 34 ▪ (0212) 522 24 24 ▪ Open daily: men 8am–10pm; women 8am–8pm ▪ Adm charge ▪ www.cagalogluhamami.com.tr

One of the city's best-known and most picturesque bathhouses, the Cağaloğlu Hamamı were built in 1741 by Sultan Mahmut I, with the intention of raising funds to support his library in Haghia Sophia. International and historical figures, from King Edward VIII and Florence Nightingale to Cameron Diaz and Harrison Ford, are all reputed to have bathed here. In more recent times, the baths have been used as a location for countless films and fashion shoots.

### 9 Soğukçeşme Sokağı
MAP R4

This steeply cobbled street, which runs between the outer walls of the Topkapı Palace and Haghia Sophia, is a sequence of pretty

---

**SÜLEYMAN I**

Known to the West as "the Magnificent", Süleyman I preferred the title Kanuni – "the law-giver". Taking the throne aged 26 in 1520, he ruled for 46 years. During that time, he doubled the size of the Ottoman Empire and, as caliph (supreme head of the Islamic faith), consolidated Sunni authority over Shia Islam. He also compiled the Codex Süleymanicus, a comprehensive legal system that defined the concept of justice, and guaranteed equal treatment for all. Süleyman was a great patron of the arts, as well as a poet and goldsmith.

Ottoman merchants' homes. The street was restored as part of a 1980s project that was one of the first of its kind in Istanbul. Nine of the houses form the Ayasofya Konakları (see p114), the city's first "special hotel", consisting of 64 guest rooms.

**10 Basilica Cistern**
(Yerebatan Sarnıcı)
MAP R4 ▪ Yerebatan Cad 13 ▪ (0212) 522 12 59 ▪ Open daily Apr–Oct: 9am–6:30pm; Nov–Mar: 9am–5:30pm ▪ Adm charge ▪ www.yerebatan.com

Known as the "Sunken Palace" in Turkish the structure had a prosaic purpose: built as a vast underground water-storage tank. Begun by Constantine, it was expanded by Justinian in 532 to ensure that Constantinople was always supplied with water; covering an area of 9,800 sq m (105,000 sq ft), it once held about 80 million litres (18 million gallons). The cistern roof is supported by 336 pillars, 8 m (26 ft) in height. Look for the upside-down Medusa heads, reused from older buildings. Istanbul's most unusual tourist attraction is also popular as a film location and a venue for concerts.

**Medusa head, Basilica Cistern**

## A DAY IN SULTANAHMET

▶ **MORNING**

Start your day at the dawn call of the *müezzin*, so that you are ready to visit the **Blue Mosque** (see pp18–19) as soon as it opens. From there, cross the square to **Haghia Sophia** (see pp16–17), then pay a visit to the **Basilica Cistern**, the **Hippodrome** (see p60) and the **Museum of Turkish and Islamic Arts** (see p61) before having a gentle stroll through the **Arasta Bazaar** (see p64) to the **Mosaic Museum** (see p64). This may sound like too much for a single morning, but the distance between each of these attractions is small, and most of the sites are fairly simple. You'll need a little time to relax after this, so choose one of the cafés or restaurants on **Divanyolu** (see p64) for lunch.

**AFTERNOON**

Now choose one of two options: either walk across to the **Topkapı Palace** and spend the whole afternoon embroiled in Ottoman court intrigue, mayhem and murder; or wander through the side streets to the **Cağaloğlu Baths** for a Turkish bath before rejoining **Soğukçeşme Sokağı** and making your way to the vast **Archaeological Museum** (see pp20–21). When you've had your fill, continue down the hill for a peaceful stroll along the waterfront at Eminönü; then take the tram back up the hill to Sultanahmet and choose one of the many rooftop bars or restaurants from which to watch the sun set over the city and the floodlights playing on Haghia Sophia and the Blue Mosque.

*See map on p61*

# Sultanahmet: The Best of the Rest

**1 Sultanahmet Square**
(Sultanahmet Meydanı)
**MAP R4**

This leafy square, once the hippodrome of Constantinople, lies between the Blue Mosque and Haghia Sophia.

**2 The Milion Monument**
(Milyon Taşi)
**MAP R4** ■ Haghia Sophia

The marble pilaster of the Milion can be found in the northern corner of Sultanahmet Square. From the 4th century AD, it was used as "point zero" for the measurement of distances to the many cities of the Byzantine Empire.

**3 Baths of Roxelana**
(Hürrem Sultan Hamamı)
**MAP R5** ■ Ayasofya Meydanı
■ (0212) 517 35 35 ■ Open 8am–10pm daily ■ www.ayasofyahamami.com

These baths were built for Süleyman the Magnificent, and are named after the sultan's apparently scheming wife.

**4 Great Palace Mosaic Museum**
(Büyük Sarayı Mozaik Müzesi)
**MAP R6** ■ Arasta Bazaar
■ (0212) 518 12 05 ■ Open 9am–6pm (summer); till 4pm (winter)
■ Adm charge

Little remains of Emperor Justinian's vast 6th-century palace except for an elaborate mosaic floor.

**Kaiser Wilhelm Fountain**

**Great Palace Mosaic Museum**

**5 Kaiser Wilhelm Fountain**
**MAP R5** ■ At Meydanı

German Emperor Wilhelm II presented this Neo-Byzantine fountain to Sultan Abdül Hamit II in 1901.

**6 Arasta Bazaar**
(Arasta Çarşısı)
**MAP R5** ■ Open 9am–9pm daily

The bazaar was originally built to provide revenue for the Blue Mosque. Today, there are around 40 shops selling carpets, textiles, jewellery and other souvenirs.

**7 Caferağa Medresesi**
**MAP R4** ■ Caferiye Sok, Soğukkuyu Çıkmazı 1 ■ (0212) 513 36 01 ■ Open 9am–7pm Mon–Sat

Watch craftspeople create art, from ceramics to calligraphy, in this 16th-century Koranic college, then take the product home or sign up for a course.

**8 Divanyolu Caddesi**
**MAP Q4**

Divanyolu was once the *Mese* – the main thoroughfare – of Byzantine Constantinople and Ottoman Istanbul, and continued all the way to the Albanian coast.

**9 Cistern of 1,001 Columns**
(Binbirdirek Sarnıcı)
**MAP Q4** ■ Binbirdirek, İmran Öktem Cad 4 ■ (0212) 518 10 01 ■ Open daily
■ Adm charge ■ www.binbirdirek.com

There are only 224 columns in this elegant 4th-century cistern. It is home to several cafés and hosts live music and events.

**10 Carpet Museum**
(Halı Müzesi)
**MAP S4** ■ Bab-ı Humayan Cad, Sultanahmet ■ (0212) 512 69 93
■ www.halimuzesi.com

The old Ottoman soup kitchen near Hagia Sophia is home to some of Anatolia's oldest carpets and kilims.

# Old City: The Best of the Rest

**(1) Haghia Eirene**
(Aya İrini Kilisesi)
MAP S4 ■ Topkapı Palace (1st courtyard) ■ (0212) 512 04 80 ■ Open 9am–4pm Tue–Sun ■ Adm charge
Built in the 6th century on the site of an earlier church, Haghia Eirene was the city's cathedral until Haghia Sophia was built. Later an Ottoman arsenal, it is now a museum and used for concerts.

**(2) Imperial Tombs**
MAP Q4 ■ Divanyolu Cad
Designed by Garabet Balyan, the tombs of three of the last Ottoman sultans, Mahmut II, Abdül Aziz and Abdül Hamid II, lie beside busy Divanyolu in a peaceful graveyard.

**(3) History of Islamic Science and Technology Museum**
MAP R2 ■ Gülhane Park ■ (0212) 528 80 65 ■ Open 9am–5pm Wed–Mon ■ Adm charge ■ www.ibttm.org
Among the exhibits at this well-laid-out museum are fantastic models of scientific inventions.

**(4) Sea Walls**
MAP M6–S6 ■ Kennedy Cad
Believed to be built by Septimius Severus and extended by Theodosius (see p77), the walls are best viewed from the main coastal road.

**(5) Church of SS Sergius and Bacchus**
(Küçük Ayasofya Camii)
MAP P6 ■ Küçük Ayasofya Camii Sok
Known as "Little Haghia Sophia", this church was built in 527 and converted into a mosque in 1500. The marble columns and carved frieze with a Greek inscription are original.

**(6) Kumkapı**
MAP M6
The old Byzantine harbour of Kumkapı is now home to a plethora of lively fish restaurants (see p67).

Ruins of the Bucoleon Palace

**(7) Bucoleon Palace**
MAP Q6 ■ Kennedy Cad
Three vast marble windows stare sightlessly out to sea from this last standing fragment of the Great Palace, built into the sea wall.

**(8) Sokollu Mehmet Paşa Mosque**
MAP P5 ■ Camii Kebir Sok ■ Open daily except during prayers; may need the keyholder to see inside the mosque
Built by Sinan for Grand Vizier Sokollu Mehmet Paşa, this lovely mosque behind the Hippodrome contains some fine İznik tiles, an elaborately painted ceiling and four tiny black stones from the Kaaba in Mecca.

**(9) Review Pavilion**
(Alay Köşkü)
MAP R3 ■ Topkapı Palace
Built into the outer walls of the Topkapı Palace, this small imperial pavilion overlooked the Sublime Porte, the entrance to the seat of government in later Ottoman times. Sultan İbrahim the Crazy took pot shots at passersby from here.

**(10) Column of the Goths**
MAP S2 ■ Gülhane Park
Erected to commemorate a great Roman victory over the Goths in the 3rd century, this fine 18-m- (60-ft-) high column is topped by an ornate Corinthian capital.

See map on p61

# Bars, Cafés and Casual Eateries

**Çorlulu Ali Paşa Medresesi**

## 1 Çorlulu Ali Paşa Medresesi
MAP Q4 ▪ Divanyolu Cad 36

Lounge on cushions in one of several atmospheric teashops with locals puffing on the *nargile*. No alcohol.

## 2 Doy-Doy
MAP Q5 ▪ Sifa Hamamı Sok 13

This cheerful place has a good selection of kebabs, pizza, salads and vegetarian options. No alcohol.

## 3 Tahiri Sultanahmet
MAP Q4 ▪ Divanyolu Cad 12

The speciality of this long-established institution is tasty meatballs with bean salad and spicy tomato sauce. It has now been surrounded by other cafés with suspiciously similar names. Make sure you find the right one!

## 4 Lale Restaurant (Pudding Shop)
MAP Q4 ▪ Divanyolu Cad 6

Once an essential stop on the "Hippy Trail", with a message board and copious quantities of cheap food, Lale has lost a little atmosphere but is still great for visitors. The food is good value, the service is friendly and they offer draught beer and free Wi-Fi.

## 5 Port Shield
MAP R3 ▪ Ebusuut Cad 2, Sirkeci

The best sports bar in the old city, Port Shield is always packed with visitors drinking the local lager, Efes Pilsen, tucking into international-style pub grub and, of course, watching the game. Flyers posted outside the pub tell you what's on.

## 6 Çaferağa Medresesi
MAP R4 ▪ Caferiye Sokak

Enjoy a cup of coffee or opt for a light meal in the courtyard of this atmospheric, Sinan-designed café, located near Haghia Sophia.

## 7 Çiğdem Pastanesi
MAP Q4 ▪ Divanyolu Cad 62

Enjoy traditional Turkish tea or a well-made cappuccino at this classic patisserie. If you're in the mood for a light snack, the sticky, honey-drenched baklava is a local favourite.

**Playing backgammon at Café Meşale**

## 8 Café Meşale
MAP R5 ▪ Arasta Bazaar

A quiet place for a cup of tea and *nargile* during the day, in the evening Café Meşale becomes a restaurant with live music and Whirling dervish performances.

## 9 Arcadia Blue Terrace Bar
MAP Q4 ▪ Dr Imran Oktem Cad 1

This bar is not the most atmospheric or best value, but the views of the old city, Bosphorus, Sea of Marmara and hills of Asia are just superb.

## 10 Yeşil Ev Beer Garden
MAP R5 ▪ Kabasakal Cad 5

Part of the Yeşil Ev Hotel, this delightful garden bar has seating in a glassed conservatory and is a great place to chill out. On offer are cakes, coffee and alcohol.

# Restaurants

**PRICE CATEGORIES**
For a typical meal of *meze* and main course for one without alcohol, and including taxes and extra charges.
.....................................................
ŧ under ŧ45  ŧŧ ŧ45–90  ŧŧŧ over ŧ90

**Starters, Seasons Restaurant**

**1 Sarnıç**
MAP R4 ▪ Soğukçeşme Sok ▪ (0212) 512 42 91 ▪ ŧŧ
The atmosphere is fabulous in this romantically converted Byzantine cistern serving Turkish/French cuisine. Book ahead.

**2 Paşazade**
MAP R3 ▪ İbn-I Kemal Cad 13, Sirkeci ▪ (0212) 513 37 57 ▪ ŧŧ
The best-value place to try recreations of Ottoman style dishes, which differ markedly from modern Turkish food. Good choice of wines.

**3 Giritli**
MAP R6 ▪ Keresteci Hakkı Sok 8 ▪ (0212) 458 22 70 ▪ ŧŧŧ
Fine fish and a bountiful array of unusual *mezes* are the stars at this Cretan-style eatery.

**Entrance to Giritli**

**4 Khorasani**
MAP Q4 ▪ Ticarethane Sok 39/41 ▪ (0212) 519 5959 ▪ ŧŧ
Khorasani's southeast Turkish specialities are delicious, with the emphasis on freshly prepared kebabs cooked over charcoal.

**5 Seasons Restaurant**
MAP R5 ▪ Four Seasons Hotel, Tevfikhane Sok 1 ▪ (0212) 402 30 00 ▪ ŧŧŧ
Top-class contemporary European cuisine with a hint of Asian fusion.

**6 Amedros**
MAP Q4 ▪ Hoca Rüstem Sok 7, off Divanyolu ▪ (0212) 522 83 56 ▪ ŧŧ
A bistro serving Turkish and European food, with good vegetarian options.

**7 Matbah**
MAP R4 ▪ Ottoman Hotel Imperial, Caferiye Sok 6 ▪ (0212) 514 61 51 ▪ ŧŧŧ
Tasty Ottoman and Turkish classics served in a lovely terrace restaurant.

**8 Balıkçı Sabahattin**
MAP R5 ▪ Seyit Hasankuyu Sok 1, off Cankurtaran Cad ▪ (0212) 458 18 24 ▪ ŧŧŧ
One of the city's finest fish restaurants since 1927.

**9 Kumkapı**
MAP M6 ▪ ŧŧ
There are many *meyhanes* (taverns) to choose from in this old fishing neighbourhood, serving fresh fish and *meze* washed down with *rakı*. Musicians play traditional *fasil* to the tables and expect to be tipped.

**10 Mozaik Restaurant**
MAP Q4 ▪ İncirli Çavuş Sok 1, off Divanyolu ▪ (0212) 512 41 77 ▪ ŧŧ
This popular restaurant serves a mix of Turkish and international favourites and is set in a restored 19th-century Ottoman house.

*See map on p61*

# 🔟 Bazaar Quarter and Eminönü

**Çemberlitaş Baths**

In 1453, following his conquest of Constantinople, Sultan Mehmet II chose this area, close to the Graeco-Roman Forum of the Bulls, as the place to begin construction of a model city based on Islamic principles. The key ingredients were mosques and *medreses* (religious schools), charitable institutions, accommodation for travellers, and a Grand Bazaar – the latter funding all the others and a great deal more besides. All these were constructed – and many still remain – in one of the city's most fascinating and vibrant districts, where you can buy, with equal ease, a plastic bucket and an antique silk carpet, an ancient religious text or a kilo of peppercorns.

**Colourful Ceramics, Grand Bazaar**

### 1 Grand Bazaar
(Kapalı Çarşı)

The bazaar was one of the first institutions established by Mehmet the Conqueror after 1453. Its oldest part is the domed İç Bedesten, a lockable warehouse used for trading and storing the most valuable wares. Today, as well as covered streets containing thousands of shops and stalls, there are cafés, restaurants and teahouses. Several hans – originally travellers' inns – are now mostly workshops and small factories (see pp22–3).

### 2 Süleymaniye Mosque
(Süleymaniye Camii)

Built for Süleyman I in 1550–57, this mosque is the largest and most lavish in the city. Süleyman and his wife Roxelana are both buried here, while the great Mimar Sinan, architect of the mosque, is buried just outside the main complex in a tomb he designed and built himself (see pp26–7).

### 3 Çemberlitaş Baths
(Çemberlitaş Hamamı)

Nurbanu, wife of the drunken Selim the Sot (son of Süleyman and Roxelana), commissioned these baths from Sinan in 1584. In those days, they were run as a charitable foundation; today they are distinctly more upmarket. Their gracious domed halls make them a popular tourist attraction (see pp30–31).

### 4 Beyazıt Square
(Beyazıt Meydanı)
MAP M3

This grand open space has been one of the city's principal meeting places for centuries. Popularly known as Beyazıt Square, its official name is Freedom Square (Hürriyet Meydanı). It stands on the site of the late Roman Forum Tauri (Forum of the Bulls), which was extended by Emperor Theodosius in 393. The forum gained its name from the bronze bull at its centre, a place of sacrifice in the pre-Christian era. Some of its colonnades were reused in the building of the Basilica Cistern (see p63), while others lie abandoned along the tram tracks on Ordu Caddesi. The square has a daily flea market, and is home to the Beyazıt Mosque and Istanbul University.

**Galata Bridge facing the New Mosque**

### (5) Galata Bridge
(Galata Köprüsü)
**MAP F3**

The predecessor of this modern bridge across the Golden Horn was an iron pontoon structure of 1909–12. It was underequipped for modern traffic and was replaced in 1994 by the current two-level concrete bridge. The city views from the lower level, especially at sunset, are breath-taking. Parts of the old bridge, further up the Golden Horn near Ayvansaray, have been re-erected.

### (6) Constantine's Column
(Çemberlitaş)
**MAP P4 ▪ Divanyolu Cad**

Built of Egyptian porphyry, this column, 35 m (115 ft) tall, once stood in the centre of the Forum of Constantine. It

**Tile detail, Rüstem Paşa Mosque**

was erected as part of the inauguration of the Roman Empire's new capital in 330. Constantine buried holy relics – said to have included the axe Noah used to build his ark – around the base. Its Turkish name, Çemberlitaş (Hooped Column), refers to the reinforcing metal hoops added in 416 and replaced in the 1970s.

### (7) Eminönü
**MAP N1**

From the Grand Bazaar, steep alleys crowded with market stalls lead down through Tahtakale to the Eminönü waterfront. It's a great place to roam, with mosques and markets, Ottoman warehouses, street sellers offering everything from *simits* to fake watches, and a bank of piers with ferries to every part of the city, all split by the swirl of traffic along the dual carriageway that leads around the coast.

### (8) Rüstem Paşa Mosque
(Rüstem Paşa Camii)
**MAP N1 ▪ Mahkeme Sok ▪ (0212) 526 73 50 ▪ Open 9am–dusk daily**

This enchanting mosque was built by Sinan in 1561. It was commissioned by Süleyman the Magnificent's daughter Mihrimah in memory of her husband, Rüstem Paşa, Süleyman's Grand Vizier. The mosque blazes with richly coloured İznik tiles, inside and out, while galleries and windows flood the hall with light.

### (9) Egyptian Bazaar
(Mısır Çarşısı)
**MAP P1 ▪ Eminönü ▪ Open 8am–7:30pm daily**

This marketplace was built in 1660 as part of the New Mosque complex. Its name derives from the fact that it was originally financed by duties on Egyptian imports, although it is better known in English as the Spice Bazaar because, for centuries, spices were the main goods sold here. These days, the bazaar has given itself over entirely to satisfying the tourist trade – it, and more, especially the streets around it, are the best place to buy small presents, from *lokum* (Turkish delight) and phials of saffron, to pistachios, almonds, incense and coffee.

## 10 New Mosque
(Yeni Cami)

**MAP P1 ■ Eminönü ■ (0212) 512 23 20 ■ Open 9am–dusk daily**

This large, rather gloomy mosque was commissioned in 1597 by Valide Sultan Safiye, mother of Sultan Mehmet III. Work was interrupted when the architect was executed for heresy and Safiye was banished after her son's death. It was completed in 1663 by Valide Sultan Turhan Hatice, mother of Sultan Mehmet IV. The interior is richly decorated but has relatively poor-quality İznik tiles.

Facing the mosque are the tombs of Valide Sultan Turhan Hatice, Mehmet IV, five other sultans and many princes and princesses.

**New Mosque**

### EMPEROR CONSTANTINE

The son of a leading army officer, Constantine (c.272–337) became one of a triumvirate of rulers of the Roman Empire. In 312, following a religious vision, he defeated his main rival, Maxentius, while fighting under the sign of the Christian cross. On becoming sole emperor in 324, he declared Christianity the state religion. In 325, he called the Council of Nicaea, which laid down the basic tenets of the faith. In 330, he inaugurated his new capital, Constantinople. On his deathbed, he formally converted to Christianity, and was buried at the city's Church of the Holy Apostles (see p75).

## A DAY'S SHOPPING

### ▶ MORNING

Start the day clean and refreshed after a visit to the **Çemberlitaş Baths** (see p69), then pop into the **Nuruosmaniye Mosque** (see p72) before getting down to the real business of the day in the **Grand Bazaar** (see p69). Take a break at one of the cafés in the bazaar and enjoy a coffee, then walk on through **Beyazıt Square** (see p69) and down the hill to **Süleymaniye Mosque** (see p69) to pay your respects at the tombs of Süleyman and Roxelana. A good option for lunch is the **Darüzziyafe** restaurant (see p73), or try one of the cafés next to the mosque.

### AFTERNOON

Leave the mosque along İsmetiye Caddesi, turn left into Uzunçarşı Caddesi and head down the hill through crowded market streets, where metal- and woodworkers still ply their trade, before turning right on **Tahtakale Caddesi**, a sensory treat with its traditional spice and coffee sellers. Carry on downhill and eventually you will end up in Eminönü, where you can visit the **Rüstem Paşa Mosque** and look at the **New Mosque** before a last round of shopping – if you have the stamina – in the **Egyptian Bazaar**. Between the New Mosque and the Egyptian Bazaar is the market for flowers, plants, seeds and songbirds. Have dinner at **Hamdi Et Lokantası** (see p73) or Paşazade near Sirkeci Station (see p67) – or take the tram back up to Sultanahmet and choose a rooftop bar or restaurant from which to enjoy sunset views.

*See map on pp68–9* ←

# The Best of the Rest

**1 Second-Hand Book Bazaar** (Sahaflar Çarşısı)

MAP M4 ▪ Sahaflar Çarşısı Sok

Manuscripts have been traded in this courtyard since medieval times, although printed books were banned until 1729. Academic textbooks and coffee table books on Turkey are now predominately sold here.

**2 Arch of Theodosius**

MAP M4 ▪ Beyazıt Meydanı

A jumble of massive, fallen columns litter the side of the road in Beyazıt Square, all that remains of the 4th-century triumphal Arch of Theodosius. The similarly carved columns in the Basilica Cistern (see p63) were clearly taken from here.

**3 Beyazıt Tower** (Beyazıt Kulesi)

MAP M3 ▪ Off Fuat Paşa Cad
▪ Closed to the public

This elegant marble tower, built in 1828 as a fire lookout, is in the Istanbul University grounds.

**4 Beyazıt Mosque** (Beyazıt Camii)

MAP M4 ▪ Ordu Cad
▪ (0212) 212 09 22

Built in 1506 for Beyazıt II, this is the oldest surviving imperial mosque in Istanbul.

**5 Atik Ali Paşa Mosque** (Atik Ali Paşa Camii)

MAP P4 ▪ Yeniçeriler Cad

This 15th-century copy of the original Fatih Mosque is named after its builder, Grand Vizier to Beyazıt II.

**6 Kalenderhane Mosque** (Kalenderhane Camii)

MAP E5 ▪ 16 Mart Şehitleri Cad ▪ Open daily except during prayer times

Built on the site of a 5th-century bathhouse, it was remodelled in the 12th century as the Church of Theotokus Kyriotissa and then into a mosque. Don't miss the superb Byzantine marble in the prayer hall.

Laleli Mosque

**7 Laleli Mosque** (Laleli Cami)

MAP D5 ▪ Ordu Cad
▪ Open prayer times only

The Laleli Mosque was built by Mustafa III in 1763, with lavish use of coloured marble in the new Ottoman Baroque style. Mustafa is buried here.

**8 Nuruosmaniye Mosque** (Nuruosmaniye Cami)

MAP P4 ▪ Vezirhanı Cad

Completed by Sultan Osman III in 1755, Nuruosmaniye was the first Ottoman Baroque mosque in the city. The mosque is part of a larger complex that includes an Islamic school and a library.

Beyazıt Tower

**9 Hodja Pasha Cultural Centre**

MAP Q2 ▪ Hoca Paşa Hamam Sok 3, Sirkeci ▪ (0212) 511 46 26

A superb setting for Whirling dervishes in a restored bathhouse.

**10 Istanbul University**

MAP M2–3 ▪ Beyazıt Meydanı
▪ (0212) 512 52 57

Turkey's oldest higher education institution, the university moved to its present campus in 1866. Security is very tight, but it is usually possible to walk through the grounds during the working week.

# Cafés and Restaurants

> **PRICE CATEGORIES**
> For a typical meal of *meze* and main
> course for one without alcohol, and
> including taxes and extra charges.
> ...................................................
> ₺ under ₺45   ₺₺ ₺45–90   ₺₺₺ over ₺90

### 1 Pandeli
MAP P1 ■ Mısır Çarşısı 1
■ (0212) 527 39 09 ■ ₺₺

Set in a domed, İznik-tiled dining room above the Spice Market, Pandeli has been an Istanbul institution since it opened in 1901. Book in advance.

### 2 Bedestan Café
MAP N3 ■ Cevahir
**Bedesteni 143–151, Kapalı Çarşı**
■ (0212) 520 22 50 ■ ₺

The most tasteful café in the Grand Bazaar *(see pp22–3)*, with snacks and both Turkish and international coffee.

### 3 Darüzziyafe
MAP M1 ■ Şifahane Cad 6
■ (0212) 511 84 14 ■ ₺₺

Once the soup kitchen of the Süleymaniye Mosque Complex, this atmospheric restaurant serves first-rate Ottoman food. No alcohol.

**Dining at Darüzziyafe**

### 4 Havuzlu Lokantası
MAP N3 ■ Gani Çelebi Sok 3,
**Kapalı Çarşı** ■ (0212) 527 33 46 ■
**Open lunch only, closed Sun** ■ ₺

This is the best of the simple restaurants in the covered bazaar, with excellent kebabs and *meze* served to the traders as well as the shoppers. Arrive early as the restaurant can get crowded.

**Refreshments at Şark Kahvesi**

### 5 Şark Kahvesi
MAP N3 ■ Yağlıkçılar Cad 134
■ (0212) 512 11 44 ■ ₺

This atmospheric café is a popular tea and coffee spot.

### 6 Tarihi Süleymaniyeli Kurufasulyeci
MAP M2 ■ Süleymaniye Cad, Prof Siddik Sami Onar Cad 11 ■ (0212) 513 62 19 ■ **No credit cards** ■ ₺

This restaurant has been serving up simple, hearty Ottoman cuisine for 80 years. Its speciality is rice and beans, slowly cooked.

### 7 Kahve Dünyası
MAP P4 ■ Nuruosmaniye
Cad 79 ■ (0212) 527 32 82 ■ ₺

Branch of the popular Turkish coffeehouse chain, close to the Grand Bazaar.

### 8 Hamdi Et Lokantası
MAP P1 ■ Kalçın Sok 17,
**Eminönü** ■ (0212) 528 03 90 ■ ₺₺₺

Specialities include *erikli kebap* (minced suckling lamb).

### 9 Surplus
MAP E3 ■ Zindan Han, Ragıp GümüşPala Cad 54 ■ (0212) 513 37 57
■ ₺₺₺

Offering great views over the city and Galata with an excellent choice of Ottoman dishes and good wines.

### 10 Nar Lokanta
MAP P3 ■ Armaggan,
Nuruosmaniye Cad 65 ■ (0212) 522 28 00 ■ ₺₺

An organic version of the traditional Turkish *lokanta*, and great for lunch.

*See map on pp68–9* ←

# TOP10 The Golden Horn, Fatih and Fener

**Mosaic, Church of Pammakaristos**

The Golden Horn, a fjord-like river inlet that divides the old and new cities of European Istanbul, is enjoying a new lease of life. Often overlooked by visitors, this part of Istanbul has almost as many minor historic attractions as the Historic Peninsula itself. Run-down Fener and Balat are now prime real-estate locations and popular settings for television programmes. The old-city shoreline has miles of narrow parks and walkways and the new city shore is home to attractions such as Miniatürk and the Rahmi Koç Museum. Plans to develop a shopping mall on the site of the old shipyards at Kasımpaşa are likely to see more change coming soon.

**AREA MAP OF THE GOLDEN HORN, FATIH AND FENER**

- **1** Top 10 Sights *see pp75–7*
- **1** Bars, Cafés and Restaurants *see p79*
- **1** The Best of the Rest *see p78*

### 1 Panorama 1453

**MAP A5 ▪ Topkapı Kültür Parkı, Topkapı ▪ (0212) 415 14 53 ▪ Open 9am–6pm daily ▪ Adm charge ▪ www.panora mikmuze.com**

Situated right by the Theodosian Walls *(see p77)*, this history museum vividly recreates the moment in 1453 when the walls were finally breached. Painted on the inside of a large dome are some 10,000 lifelike figures replaying the desperate Byzantine defence against the besieging Ottoman Turks. Take a seat in the museum's helicopter simulator for a bird's-eye view of Istanbul or a historical tour around the country.

**Aqueduct of Valens**

### 2 Church of Pammakaristos (Fethiye Camii)

**MAP K3 ▪ Fethiye Kapısı Sok ▪ Open 9am–5pm daily ▪ Adm charge**

Built by Emperor John II Comnenus in the 12th century, this was the headquarters of the Greek Orthodox Patriarchate from 1456 to 1568. The church was later converted into a mosque, and in 1573 renamed Fethiye (Victory) to celebrate Murat III's conquest of present-day Georgia and Azerbaijan. The side-chapel is a museum, containing some of the finest Byzantine mosaics in Istanbul.

### 3 Aqueduct of Valens (Bozdoğan Kemeri)

**MAP D4 ▪ Atatürk Bulvarı (north side of Saraçhane Parkı)**

West of Süleymaniye are the remains of the two-storey aqueduct built by Emperor Valens in 368. Repaired many times in the intervening years, it remained in use until the 19th century, bringing water from the Belgrade Forest to the centre of the Great Palace complex.

### 4 Fatih Mosque (Fatih Camii)

**MAP C3–4 ▪ Fevzi Paşa Cad ▪ Open 9am–dusk daily**

This huge Baroque mosque is the third building to have occupied this site. The first was the Church of the Holy Apostles (burial place of many Byzantine emperors, including Constantine). Mehmet the Conqueror then constructed Istanbul's first great imperial mosque here, but it was destroyed in an earthquake in 1766. Today's mosque was built mainly in the 18th century by Sultan Mustafa III. The grounds contain the tombs of Mehmet the Conqueror and his wife Gülbahar Hatun. On Wednesdays there is a colourful market in the surrounding streets.

**Fatih Mosque**

**Grounds of Yedikule Castle**

### (5) Yedikule Castle
(Yedikule Hisarı)

MAP A6 ▪ Yedikule Meydanı Sok
▪ Open 9am–6:30pm (summer);
till 4:30pm (winter) ▪ Adm charge

This seven-tower Ottoman fortress is
built onto a section of the Theodosian
Walls. Built within its outer walls,
is the well known Golden Gate, a
triumphal arch, constructed by
Emperor Theodosius I in 390.

**Pierre Loti Café**

### (6) Pierre Loti
During his time in Istanbul,
Pierre Loti – the pseudonym and nom
de plume of French sailor, author and
Turkophile Julien Viaud – frequented
a café in Eyüp, and the surrounding
area is now named after him. Arriving
in the city in 1876, Viaud fell in love
with a local woman whose name he
gave to the title of his novel, *Aziyade*,
which chronicles their difficult rela-
tionship. The area known as Pierre
Loti Hill can be visited via the cable
car beside Eyüp Mosque. The hilltop
Pierre Loti Café *(see p79)* affords
splendid views of the Golden Horn.

### (7) Eyüp Sultan Mosque
(Eyüp Sultan Camii)

MAP A4 ▪ Eyüp Meydanı (off Camii
Kebir Cad) ▪ (0212) 564 73 68 ▪ Tomb
open 9:30am–4:30pm ▪ Donations

Istanbul's holiest mosque was built
by Mehmet the Conqueror in 1458,
over the *türbe* (burial site) of the
Prophet Mohammed's friend and
standard-bearer, Eyüp el-Ensari,
whose tomb opposite is one of the
holiest pilgrimage sites in Islam (after
Mecca and Jerusalem). The mosque
courtyard, where the coronations of
Ottoman sultans took place, has
intricately painted İznik tiles, and is
usually filled with worshippers
queuing to pay their respects.

### (8) Church of St Saviour in Chora (Kariye Camii)

First a church, then a mosque, now
a museum, the Church of St Saviour
in Chora was rebuilt in the late 11th
century and restored in the early
14th by Theodore Metochites, who
also commissioned the superb
series of mosaics and frescoes that
he hoped would secure him "a
glorious memory among posterity till
the end of the world" *(see pp28–9)*.

### (9) Rahmi Koç Museum
(Rahmi Koç Müzesi)

MAP A5 ▪ Hasköy Cad 5 ▪ (0212) 369
66 00 ▪ Open Apr–Sep: 10am–5pm
Tue–Fri, 10am–8pm Sat & Sun; Oct–
Mar: 8am–5pm Tue–Fri, 10am–6pm
Sat & Sun ▪ Adm charge ▪
www.rmk-museum.org.tr

This eclectic museum is named
after its founder, the industrialist

Rahmi Koç. The main part of the collection – a magnificent assortment of vintage cars, steam engines, motorbikes, boats, the imperial railway carriage of Sultan Abdül Aziz, and much more besides – is situated in a 19th-century shipyard building. Outside are aircraft, boats, restored shops and a submarine. Across the road, in a restored Ottoman anchor foundry with Byzantine foundations, are model engines, trains, cars and more boats. There is also an excellent café *(see p79)* and the gourmet Halat Restaurant.

**Vintage car**

### ⑩ Theodosian Walls
(Teodos II Surları)

**MAP A5**

Built by Emperor Theodosius II in 412–22, the walls enclosing the old city from the Sea of Marmara (Yedikule) to the Golden Horn (Ayvansaray) are startlingly intact. You can walk sections, especially at Yedikule *(see p65)*, although some isolated stretches are not safe to visit alone. The moat has been turned into a vegetable garden.

**BUILT TO LAST**

There were 10 fortified gates and 192 towers in the Theodosian Walls. The outer wall is 2-m (6-ft) thick and 8.5-m (28-ft) tall, separated from the 5-m- (16-ft-) thick, 12-m- (39-ft-) high inner wall by a 20-m (66-ft) moat (below). The walls of Byzantium were built to withstand anything, and did so for 1,000 years. When they were breached in 1453, the last Byzantine Emperor, Constantine XI, vanished into history, last seen fighting on the wall itself.

**A DAY ALONG THE GOLDEN HORN**

▶ **MORNING**

Take the **Haliç ferry** from near the Galata Bridge to **Eyüp**, then ride the cable car up the tree-clad cemetery hill. Enjoy tea at **Pierre Loti Café** *(see p79)* before heading down through the cemetery to queue at the tomb of Eyüp Ensari in the **Eyüp Sultan Mosque**. Stroll down the Golden Horn to join the line of the **Theodosian Walls**. Turn south and walk alongside the mighty walls as they march uphill to the **Palace of the Porphyrogenitus** *(see p78)*. Deviate slightly from the line of the walls to visit the Byzantine **Church of St Saviour in Chora**, with its superb mosaics and frescoes. Right next to the church the **Asitane Restaurant** *(see p79)* serves up delicious Ottoman Turkish dishes in a leafy garden.

**AFTERNOON**

Continue south along the line of the walls, admiring the defences which kept the city's enemies at bay for centuries. The first high-light en route is the **Mihrimah Mosque**, spectacularly situated on the old city's highest hill. About halfway along the length of the walls is **Panorama 1453** *(see p75)*, with its recreation of the famous siege of 1453. Continue downhill to **Yedikule Fortress**, a massive Ottoman-era fortress incorporating part of the Theodosian walls and the legendary Golden Gate. Climb up one of its towers for views of the Sea of Marmara. The total length of the walk is around 6 km (4 miles); ride the metro back to the centre from the Kazlıçeşme stop.

*See map on p74*

# The Best of the Rest

### 1 Church of the Pantocrator
(Molla Zeyrek Camii)
**MAP D3** ■ İbadethane Sok, Küçükpazar
■ (0212) 532 50 23 ■ Bus 28, 61B, 87
■ Open 20 mins before and after prayer times ■ Small tips welcomed

This 12th-century Byzantine church was converted into a mosque in 1453.

### 2 Aynalıkavak Palace
(Aynalıkavak Kasrı)
**MAP D1** ■ Aynalikavak Cad, Hasköy
■ (0212) 256 95 70 ■ Bus 47, 54
■ Open 9am–5pm daily except Mon & Thu ■ Adm charge

This 17th-century Ottoman palace has an interesting exhibition of Turkish musical instruments.

### 3 Church of St Stephen of the Bulgars
(Bulgar Kilisesi)
**MAP D2** ■ Mürsel Paşa Cad 85, Balat
■ Bus 55T, 99A ■ Open 9am–5pm daily

The body of this late 19th-century church was entirely prefabricated in Vienna, in cast iron.

### 4 Yavuz Selim Mosque
(Yavuz Selim Camii)
**MAP C3** ■ Yavuz Selim Cad, Fatih
■ Bus 90 ■ Tomb open 9am–5pm

This elegant 16th-century mosque was built to honour Selim I, who doubled the size of the Ottoman Empire. His tomb is in the garden.

### 5 Church of St George
(Ortodoks Parikhanesi)
**MAP L3** ■ Sadrazam Ali Paşa Cad 35, Fener ■ (0212) 525 54 16 ■ Bus 55T, 99A ■ Open 9am–5pm daily

This church is the spiritual centre of the Orthodox Church community.

### 6 Balat
**MAP K2** ■ Synagogue: Gevgili Sok ■ (0212) 244 19 80 ■ Bus 55T, 99A
■ Open by appointment

Balat was once home to the city's Sephardic Jewish community. Don't miss out on the 15th-century Ahrida Synagogue, which is one of the oldest in Istanbul.

### 7 Church of St Mary of the Mongols (Kanlı Kilise)
**MAP L3** ■ Tevkii Cafer Mektebi Sok, Fener ■ (0212) 521 71 39 ■ Bus 55T, 99A ■ Ring on the compound door for entry

This beautiful church was built by Maria Palaeologina, a Byzantine princess who married a Mongol khan, and later became a nun.

### 8 Palace of the Porphyrogenitus
(Tekfur Sarayı)
**MAP J1** ■ Şişhane Cad, Edirnekapı
■ Bus 87, 90, 126 ■ Ferry Haliç to Ayvansaray ■ Groups only, by appointment with Haghia Sophia

Once an annexe of the Blachernae Palace, it has recently been restored.

### 9 Eyüp Cemetery
**MAP A4** ■ Camii Kebir Sok
■ Bus 39, 55T, 99A ■ Ferry Haliç to Eyüp

A steep uphill walk leads past hundreds of Ottoman-era gravestones. There's a superb view of the Golden Horn.

### 10 Miniatürk
**MAP A4** ■ İmrahor Cad, Sütlüce
■ Bus 47C, 47E ■ Ferry Haliç to Sütlüce
■ Open 9am–7pm daily (9pm in high season) ■ Adm charge

This intriguing park contains 1:25 scale models of the country's most impressive structures, from the Bosphorus Bridge to Haghia Sophia.

**Miniature models at Miniatürk**

# Bars, Cafés and Restaurants

**PRICE CATEGORIES**

For a typical meal of *meze* and main course for one without alcohol, and including taxes and extra charges.
...............................................................
₺ under ₺45  ₺₺ ₺45–90  ₺₺₺ over ₺90

**1 Café du Levant, Sütlüce**

MAP A4 ■ Hasköy Cad 5
■ (0212) 369 66 07 ■ ₺₺

This café is located in the Rahmi Koç museum *(see p76)* and serves stylish Gallic cuisine.

**2 Pierre Loti Café, Eyüp**

MAP A4 ■ Gümüşsuyu Karyağdı Sok 5 ■ (0212) 497 13 13 ■ ₺

The interior of this hilltop café has traditional tiles, tea-making paraphernalia and exhibits relating to the novelist Pierre Loti *(see p76)*. Outside, the shady terrace offers fine views of the Goldern Horn.

**3 Cibalikapı Balıkçısı, Fener**

MAP E3 ■ Kadir Has Cad 5
■ (0212) 533 28 46 ■ ₺₺

This traditional tavern serves fresh fish of the day and a wonderful selection of hot and cold *meze*. Lively and informal with good views of the Golden Horn.

**4 Barba Giritli Balık Lokantası, Fener**

MAP E3 ■ Kadir Has Cad 3
■ (0212) 533 18 66 ■ ₺₺

This two-storey restaurant offers excellent fish and *meze* dishes that include *hamsi* (anchovies) and *ezme* (hot pepper dip).

**5 Köfteci Arnavut, Balat**

MAP L2 ■ Mürselpaşa Cad 139
■ (0212) 531 66 52 ■ ₺

Serving up *köfte* (meatballs) since 1947, this little eatery is the perfect place to stop for a traditional Turkish lunch. The doors close when the *köfte* run out, usually by mid-afternoon, so get there early.

**Dish at Asitane Restaurant**

**6 Asitane Restaurant, Edirnekapı**

MAP J2 ■ Kariye Oteli, Kariye Camii Sok 6 ■ (0212) 635 79 97 ■ ₺₺

Dishes with delicate Ottoman flavours are served in a classy setting, with a summer courtyard. Reservations are recommended.

**7 Ottoman Restaurant, Fener**

MAP E3 ■ Kadir Has Cad 11, Cibali
■ (0212) 631 75 67 ■ ₺₺

Ottoman *beğendi* – grilled lamb on aubergine cooked with cream and spices – comes with fine views.

**8 Siirt Şeref Büryan, Fatih**

MAP C4 ■ Itfaye Cad 4 ■ (0212) 635 80 85 ■ ₺₺

An authentic eatery specializing in *perde pilaf*, a delicious pilau rice cooked in pastry, and *büryan*, lamb slow-cooked in a clay pit. No alcohol.

**9 Kömür, Fatih**

MAP J3 ■ Fevziy Paşa Cad 18
■ (0212) 631 40 04 ■ ₺

Locals flock to this simple café for delicious and ultra-cheap self-service dishes of Black Sea food.

**10 Zeyrekhane Restaurant, Fatih**

MAP D3 ■ İbadethane Sok 10, Zeyrek
■ (0212) 532 27 78 ■ Open daily ■ ₺₺

Ottoman food is served on a terrace with fine views of the old city. Booking is advised.

*See map on p74*

# TOP 10 Beyoğlu

**Gold shield in the Military Museum**

Set on a steep hill north of the Golden Horn, facing the old town of Stamboul, is the "new town" of Beyoğlu, previously known as Pera – simply, "the other side". The area is hardly "new"; there has been a settlement here for 2,000 years. In the early Byzantine era, Pera was populated by Jewish merchants. In the late 13th century, Genoese merchants were given Galata as a reward for helping the Byzantines recapture the city from the Crusaders. In Ottoman times, European powers established embassies and trading centres, and Istanbul's commercial centre shifted here from the Grand Bazaar area. Today, Beyoğlu is the heart of modern European Istanbul, its streets (such as pedestrianized İstiklal Caddesi) lined with consulates, churches, stylish bars and all the latest shops.

## 1 Galata Tower
### (Galata Kulesi)
MAP F2 ■ Büyük Hendek Sok ■ (0212) 293 81 80 ■ Viewing platform open 9am–7pm daily (dinner show from 8pm–1am) ■ Adm charge

One of the city's most distinctive sights, the 67-m- (220-ft-) high tower was built in 1348 by the Genoese, the Byzantine Empire's greatest trading partners, as part of their fortification of Galata. Since then, the tower has survived several earthquakes, and been restored many times. A lift climbs eleven floors to the top where there is a viewing balcony, nightclub and restaurant – views of the Golden Horn and the city are fabulous. In the evenings, the restaurant hosts a dinner and cabaret with Turkish folk dance and belly dancing *(see p88)*.

**Galata Tower**

*Previous pages* The Golden Horn as seen from Galata Tower

## AREA MAP OF BEYOĞLU

**1** Top 10 Sights
*see pp82–5*

**1** Bars, Cafés &
Restaurants *see p89*

**1** İstiklal Caddesi
*see p86*

**1** Shopping
*see p87*

**1** Nightlife
*see p88*

0 metres 200
0 yards 200

### **2** Pera Palace Hotel
(Pera Palas Oteli)

**MAP J5 ▪ Meşrutiyet Cad 52 ▪ (0212)
337 40 00 ▪ www.perapalace.com**

Opened in 1895 mainly for travellers
on the *Orient Express*, the Pera
Palace is Istanbul's most famous
hotel. British thriller writer Agatha
Christie stayed here often between
1924 and 1933 and is said to have
written *Murder on the Orient Express*
in Room 411. Over the years, the
hotel has also been frequented by
well-known figures such as Mata
Hari, Leon Trotsky, Greta Garbo and
Atatürk, the "Father of the Turks"
(*see p33*). In 1981, the Atatürk

Museum was opened in the great
leader's favourite room in the hotel,
No. 101. The exhibit displays many of
his personal items.

### **3** İstiklal Caddesi
**MAP J6–L4**

Packed with shoppers by day,
Beyoğlu's main street (*see p86*) is
also an entertainment hub by night
and home to several interesting
sights. It is pedestrianized, but you
can hop on the tram, which runs the
street's entire length. Be aware that
many protests and demonstrations
take place here. Visitors are advised
to stay well away from them.

###  Mevlevi Monastery
(Mevlevi Tekkesi)

**MAP J6** ■ **Galip Dede Cad 15**
■ **(0212) 245 41 41** ■ **Open 9am–4pm
Wed–Mon** ■ **Adm charge; book in
advance for dancing**

This late 18th-century monastery
belonged to a Sufi sect of Islamic
mystics and is now the Whirling
Dervish Museum (Mevlevihane
Müzesi). Sufi Whirling Dervishes
still dance here on Sundays; look
out for times on a board outside.
The museum contains many
artifacts associated with dervish
rituals, such as begging bowls and
musical instruments, but star of the
show is the beautiful *semahane*, or
ritual dance hall, upstairs.

###  Military Museum
(Askeri Müze)

**MAP B4** ■ **Vali Konağı Cad, Harbiye**
■ **(0212) 233 27 20** ■ **Open 9am–5pm
Wed–Sun (Mehter Band 3pm daily)**
■ **Adm charge**

Housed in the former military
academy where Atatürk was
educated, the museum contains
thousands of exhibits telling the
story of warfare from Ottoman times
to World War II. Chain mail, armour,
swords and embroidered tents are
on display; one room is devoted to
Atatürk's career. A highlight is the
show by the Mehter Band, recreating
the military music of the Janissaries,
the elite Ottoman corps.

###  Taksim Square
(Taksim Meydanı)

**MAP L4**

The busy hub of modern
Beyoğlu, Taksim Square was
the end of the water supply
line laid down by Mahmut I
in 1732 – his original stone
reservoir still stands at
the square's western end.
On the same side of the
square is the Monument
of Independence, a
patriotic sculpture
of Atatürk and other
revolutionary heroes
erected in 1928.

**Monument of
Independence**

---

**MILITARY MARCHES**

The Mehter music performed daily in
the grounds of the Military Museum
has been widely influential. Founded
in the 14th century during the reign
of Osman I, the Ottoman Janissary
bands accompanied the army as it
marched to war, intimidating the
enemy through the sheer volume of
their huge drums, cymbals and *zurnas*
(traditional reed instruments). The
rousing military style of Mehter music
strongly influenced the compositions
of Beethoven and Mozart, as well as
the da Souza military marches played
by today's brass bands.

###  Museum of Innocence
(Masümiyet Müzesi)

**MAP K6** ■ **Dalgiç Cıkmaz 2, Çukurcuma**
■ **(0212) 252 97 38** ■ **Open 10am–6pm
Tue–Sun (until 9pm Thu)** ■ **Adm
charge** ■ **www.masumiyetmuzesi.org**

Nobel-prize-winning Turkish author
Orhan Pamuk's book *The Museum
of Innocence* is the inspiration for
this hip museum. The thousands
of cigarette butts that the angst-
ridden protagonist of the novel
smoked are on display, along with
other ephemera, all exhibited in a
converted period town house.

###  Çukurcuma
**MAP K5**

The old quarter of Beyoğlu is today
a centre for second-hand and
antiques trades. Its mansions
and warehouses have been
beautifully restored, and this
is now a great place to browse
for anything from antique
cabinets to modern upholstery
materials or 1960s comics.

###  Church of SS
Peter and Paul
(Sen Piyer Kilisesi)

**MAP F3** ■ **Galata Kulesi
Sok 44, Karaköy** ■ **(0212)
249 23 85** ■ **Open
10:30am–noon Sun**

When their original
church was requisi-
tioned as a mosque in

the early 16th century, the Dominican brothers of Galata moved to this site, just below the Galata Tower. The church was built in the style of a basilica with four side-altars. It also has a blue cupola studded with gold stars over the choir. Mass is said here in Italian every morning. Ring the bell by the tiny door (accessed through the courtyard) to gain admittance.

*The Tortoise Trainer* (1906), Pera Museum

## 10 Pera Museum
(Pera Müzesi)

MAP J5 ▪ Meşrutiyet Cad 65 ▪ (0212) 334 99 00 ▪ Open 10am–7pm Tue–Sat (to 10pm Fri), noon–6pm Sun ▪ Adm charge

The old Bristol Hotel has been revived as the home of this museum and gallery, privately run by the Suna and İnan Kiraç Foundation set up by wealthy Turkish industrialists. The first two floors display the Kiraç family's collections of Kutahya tiles and ceramics and Anatolian weights and measures. The next floor has an intriguing collection, most of it by European artists, detailing life at the Ottoman imperial court from the 17th century onwards. The top storeys are given over to temporary shows.

## A DAY IN BEYOĞLU

Military Museum (1.2km) — Taksim Square
Nevizade Sokak
Church of Saint Anthony of Padua — Galatasaray High School
İstiklal Caddesi — Galatasaray Baths — Çukurcuma
Beyoğlu İş Merkezi
Asmalı Mescit Sokağı — Church of St Mary Draperis
Mevlevi Monastery
Galata Tower — Galip Dede Caddesi

### ▶ MORNING

Walk over the Galata Bridge and head up to the **Galata Tower** (see p82). Take the lift to the top to walk the perimeter balcony and enjoy the breathtaking view. Back at the bottom, refresh yourself at a traditional tea garden before taking a leisurely stroll up **Galip Dede Caddesi** (see p87) to peer into the music shops and have a go on a traditional Turkish instrument if the fancy takes you. Continue on towards **Tünel** (see p86) and learn about the Whirling dervishes at the **Mevlevi Monastery**. For lunch, try a small street café on bohemian **Asmalı Mescit Sokağı**, or go Gallic on Fransız Sokağı (French Street).

### AFTERNOON

Walk up **İstiklal Caddesi** (see p86) browsing the music shops, fashion stores and **Beyoğlu İş Merkezi** (see p87), then visit the **Church of St Mary Draperis** and the **Church of Saint Anthony of Padua** (see p86). Get to the **Military Museum** in time for the 3pm performance by the Mehter Band. Head to **Çukurcuma** via **Taksim Square**, stopping off for some refreshments if you need to. After browsing the vast array of antique shops in Çukurcuma, relax at the **Galatasaray Baths** (see p86). Refreshed, wander past the **Galatasaray High School** (see p86) and cut through to boisterous **Nevizade Sokak** (see p89) to choose a place to wine and dine. Fish is the speciality here – start with a few *meze* then try the catch of the day, washing it down with a glass of *rakı*.

See map on p83

# İstiklal Caddesi

### ① Tünel
**MAP J6**

The 573-m (1,880-ft) Tünel is a funicular that runs up the steep slope from Galata Bridge to Beyoğlu. Built by the French in 1874, it is one of the world's oldest metros.

### ② Christ Church
**MAP J6 ▪ Serdar Ekrem Sok 52 ▪ (0212) 251 56 16**

The centre of the Anglican community in Istanbul, this church was consecrated in 1868 as the Crimean Memorial Church, using English money and Maltese stone.

**Galatasaray Baths**

### ③ Galatasaray Baths (Tarihi Galatasaray Hamamı)
**MAP K5 ▪ Turnacıbaşı Sok 24 (off İstiklal Cad) ▪ (0212) 252 42 42 (men) & (0212) 249 43 42 (women) ▪ Open 7am–10pm (men), 8am–9pm (women) daily ▪ Adm charge**

Wealthy Istanbulites come here to be sweated, scrubbed and scraped in one of the finest *hamams* in Istanbul, built by Beyazit II in 1481. Today the baths are fully modernized but still retain their charm. Men and women bathe separately.

### ④ Church of St Anthony of Padua
**MAP J5 ▪ İstiklal Cad 171 ▪ (0212) 244 09 35 ▪ Open 8am–7:30pm daily (closed 12:30–3pm Sun)**

This red-brick Neo-Gothic building is the largest working Catholic church in the city. The church was built in 1911 by Istanbul-born Italian architect Giulio Mongeri.

### ⑤ Swedish Consulate
**MAP J6 ▪ İstiklal Cad 497 ▪ (0212) 334 06 00 ▪ Open for events only**

Built in 1757, this magnificent embassy was reconstructed after a fire in 1870.

### ⑥ Yapı Kredi Vedat Nedim Tör Müzesi
**MAP J5 ▪ İstiklal Cad 285 ▪ (0212) 252 47 00 ▪ Open 10am–6:45pm Mon–Fri, 10am–5:45pm Sat, 1–5:45pm Sun**

This smart art gallery was set up by one of Turkey's largest banks.

### ⑦ Galatasaray High School (Galatasaray Lisesi)
**MAP K5 ▪ İstiklal Cad 159 ▪ (0212) 249 11 00 ▪ Closed to the public**

Originally founded by Sultan Beyazıt II in 1481 to train imperial pages, this is still Turkey's premier school.

### ⑧ Fish Market (Balık Pazarı)
**MAP J5**

A fish, fruit and veg market by day, by night the adjacent alleys are filled with cheap and lively restaurants.

### ⑨ Flower Arcade (Çiçek Pasajı)
**MAP K4**

Housed in the Cité de Pera (1876), one of several ornate Victorian arcades along İstiklal, this former flower market is now an entertaining (if touristy) tavern quarter.

### ⑩ Nostalgic Tram
**MAP J5–L4**

The horse-drawn tram service that rumbled along İstiklal Caddesi in the 19th century was electrified in 1914 (the horses were taken off to war). The service closed in 1961, but was revived in 1990. Its red carriages have become an icon of Beyoğlu. Buy tickets at either end of the line.

# Shopping

**1 Aznavur Pasajı**
MAP K5 ▪ İstiklal Cad 108, Galatasaray Meydanı

This Italian-style arcade has been on İstiklal Caddesi since 1883. You can buy a range of handmade goods here, including jewellery, clothes and souvenirs, on any of the nine floors.

**2 Galip Dede Caddesi**
MAP J6 ▪ Tünel

Musical instruments, such as the traditional *oud*, handmade violins and locally made cymbals, are sold at a string of specialist music shops in this small street.

**3 Çukurcuma**
MAP K5

The streets between Cihangir and Galatasaray form part of the old quarter and are the best spots for antique-hunting *(see p84)*.

**4 Avrupa Pasajı**
MAP J5 ▪ Meşrutiyet Cad 16

The 22 shops in this quiet, attractive old arcade carry a fine selection of jewellery, ceramics and other traditional Turkish crafts. There are also quirkier souvenirs such as old prints and maps.

**5 Beyoğlu İş Merkezi**
MAP J5 ▪ İstiklal Cad 187

A haven for bargain-hunters, the three-storey Beyoğlu İş Merkezi is filled with tiny shops selling mainly high-street fashion labels. Many of the products here are second-hand or surplus; hence the rock-bottom prices. A tailor's shop in the basement can make alterations on the same day.

**6 Koton**
MAP K4 ▪ İstiklal Cad 54 in Demirören AVM

You'll find both men's and women's fashions at this reasonably priced Turkish chain store. Designs are updated regularly and include party- and daywear.

**Homer Books**

**7 Homer Books**
MAP K5 ▪ Yeni Çarşi Cad 12/A, Beyoğlu

One of the best-stocked bookshops in the city, with English-language titles on all matters Istanbul and Turkey. English-speaking staff, too.

**8 Mavi Jeans**
MAP K5 ▪ İstiklal Cad 117

Jeans made from organic cotton and hip Istanbul T-shirts are among the stylish items available from one of Turkey's most popular fashion brands.

**9 Paşabahçe**
MAP J5 ▪ İstiklal Cad 314

The flagship showroom of one of the world's largest glass manufacturers sells affordable modern and traditional glassware, all made in Turkey.

**10 Ali Muhiddin Hacı Bekir**
MAP K4 ▪ İstiklal Cad 83A

The place for *lokum* (Turkish delight), this is the Beyoğlu branch of the confectioners who invented the stuff in 1777. Other treats include *akide* (boiled sweets), *helva* and baklava.

***Lokum* at Ali Muhiddin Hacı Bekir**

*See map on p83*

# Nightlife

**Nardis Jazz Club**

### 1 Nardis Jazz Club
MAP F3 ■ Kuledibi Sok 14
■ (0212) 244 63 27

There's live music every night. Find a table near the stage and choose from the menu of salads and pasta.

### 2 Babylon
MAP J6 ■ Şeyhbender Sok 3
■ (0212) 292 73 68 ■ www.babylon.com.tr

Babylon is indisputably the city's best venue for live music of every kind.

### 3 Al Jamal
MAP B4 ■ Taşkışla Cad 13, Maçka ■ (0212) 296 09 69

Stretch out on the chandelier-lit sofa seating and splash out for quality belly dancing (including male dancers in drag) and fine food. Al Jamal attracts high-rolling Turks rather than the usual tourists, and offers a more authentic experience.

### 4 Indigo
MAP J5 ■ İstiklal Cad, Akarsu Sok 1–5 ■ (0212) 244 85 67

With a resident DJ and live guest acts, this dimly lit club is geared up for serious lovers of electronic music.

**Indigo nightclub**

### 5 Süheyla
MAP J4 ■ Kalyoncu Kulluk Cad 19 (behind Balık Pazarı)
■ (0212) 251 83 47

Süheyla is one of the best places to hear *fasıl* – the music of the meyhanes (see p110), part Turkish classical, part wild Gypsy. The set menu includes unlimited *rakı*.

### 6 Minimuzikhol
MAP L5 ■ Soğancı Sok 7, off Sıraselviler Cad ■ (0212) 245 19 96

Small, lively club attracting discerning clubbers who come for the techno, dubstep and hip-hop. Attracts internationally acclaimed DJs on occasion.

### 7 Garaj Istanbul
MAP K5 ■ Kaymakam Reşat Bey Sok 11A, off Yeni Çarşı Cad ■ (0212) 244 44 99

Tucked away on a Beyoğlu backstreet, this club offers an adventurous programme of theatre performances, live bands and other cultural events.

### 8 360
MAP J5 ■ İstikal Cad 163
■ (0212) 251 10 42

The beautiful people flock to this rooftop terrace with superb views. The club offers lounge music with dinner, and a resident DJ for a funkier dance sound after midnight.

### 9 Peyote
MAP J4 ■ Kameriye Sok 4, off Hamalbaşı Cad ■ (0212) 251 43 98

This popular local venue for alternative and world-music bands draws a hip, young crowd with its low prices and up-and-coming acts.

### 10 Salon İKSV
MAP J6 ■ Sadi Konuralp Cad 5, off Refik Saydam Cad
■ (0212) 334 07 00

An intimate venue for classical, jazz, world music, as well as dance and theatre. Traditional dramas performed here get a modern twist.

# Bars, Cafés and Restaurants

### 1 Galata House
MAP F2 ■ Galata Kulesi Sok 15 ■ (0212) 245 18 61 ■ Closed Mon ■ ₺₺

Galata House is a true original – a restaurant in a converted British jail. It serves delicious Russian-Georgian-Turkish food.

**Galata House**

### 2 Nevizade Sokak
MAP K4 ■ ₺₺

Several little fish restaurants on one tiny street serve the catch of the day, washed down with rakı.

### 3 Kafe Ara
MAP J5 ■ Tosbağa Sok 8, off Yeni Çarşı Cad ■ (0212) 245 41 05 ■ ₺₺

There's an intellectual, artistic vibe at this café serving fresh, light food (but no alcohol). It is decorated with the work of Turkey's most famous photographer, Ara Güler.

### 4 Refik
MAP J6 ■ Sofyali Sok 6–8 ■ (0212) 243 28 34 ■ ₺₺

A true meyhane with meze, free-flowing wine and a bohemian clientele, Refik is stuck in the past and all the better for it.

### 5 Yakup 2
MAP J6 ■ Asmalı Mescit Sok 35 ■ (0212) 249 29 25 ■ ₺

Yakup 2 has a smoky, alcohol-rich atmosphere popular with large groups. The food here is excellent, with a wide choice of hot and cold meze, salads and grills.

**PRICE CATEGORIES**

For a typical meal of meze and main course for one without alcohol, and including taxes and extra charges.

₺ under ₺45  ₺₺ ₺45–90  ₺₺₺ over ₺90

### 6 Mandabatmaz
MAP J5 ■ Olivia Geçidi, off İstiklal Cad ■ ₺

Sit on low stools in this hole-in-the-wall café to drink Istanbul's very best, rich and aromatic Turkish coffee at a bargain price.

### 7 Leb-i-Derya
MAP J6 ■ Kumbaracı Yokuşu 57/6 ■ (0212) 293 49 89 ■ ₺₺

Start with a cocktail, then sample their speciality, the 40-spiced steak Mahmudiye. Come early if you want to eat on the tiny roof terrace. Reservations essential at weekends.

### 8 Zencefil
MAP K4 ■ Kurabiye Sok 8–10 ■ (0212) 243 82 34 ■ ₺

Light, tasty vegetarian food in European style is on offer at this lovely little café-restaurant with a summer garden.

### 9 Sensus
MAP F2 ■ Büyük Hendek Cad 5, Galata ■ (0212) 245 56 57 ■ ₺₺

This trendy basement wine bar stocks dozens of different Turkish wines and a range of cheeses to go with them. Packed weekend nights.

### 10 Meze by Lemon Tree
MAP J6 ■ Meşrutiyet Cad 83/B, Beyoğlu ■ (0212) 252 83 02 ■ ₺₺₺

The traditional Turkish meyhane is given a contemporary makeover in this stylish restaurant.

**Hummus, Meze by Lemon Tree**

The meze here are superb. Book well in advance for weekend evenings.

*See map on p83*

# 🔟 The Bosphorus

**Sultan's throne, Naval Museum**

The Bosphorus is one of the world's busiest waterways, part of the only shipping lane from the Black Sea to the Mediterranean. Just 32-km (20-miles) long and varying in width from 3.5 km (about 2.2 miles) to 698 m (2,290 ft), it connects the Black Sea to the Sea of Marmara, dividing Europe from Asia. The straits are governed by international maritime law, so Turkey has authority only over vessels flying a Turkish flag. Navigation can be difficult, since the mixture of fresh water from the Black Sea and salt water from the Sea of Marmara creates complex cross-currents. All of this is fascinating, but to most of us what really counts is the beauty of the waterway and the historic buildings that line its shores.

## AREA MAP OF THE BOSPHORUS

1. **Top 10 Sights**
   see pp91–3

2. **Bars, Cafés & Restaurants** see p95

3. **The Best of the Rest** see p94

Istanbul Modern gallery

### ① Istanbul Modern
(Istanbul Modern)

MAP G2 ■ Meclis-i Mebusan Cad, Karaköy ■ (0212) 334 73 00 ■ Open 10am–6pm Tue–Sun (to 8pm Thu) ■ Adm charge ■ www.istanbulmodern.org

This cutting-edge gallery's small collection of modern Turkish painting, sculpture and photography is augmented by touring exhibitions, video and audio installations, and an arthouse cinema (see p44).

### ② Dolmabahçe Palace
(Dolmabahçe Sarayı)

In 1856, Sultan Abdül Mecit removed his entire family and government from the Topkapı to this European-style palace at Beşiktaş on the Bosphorus shore (see pp32–3).

### ③ Naval Museum
(Deniz Müzesi)

MAP C5 ■ Hayrettin Paşa İskelesi Sok, Beşiktaş ■ (0212) 327 43 45 ■ Tram Kabataş then 5-min walk ■ Open 9am–5pm Wed–Fri, 10am–6pm Sat & Sun (summer) ■ Adm charge

Ottoman Turkey's great maritime history is celebrated in this state-of-the-art museum splendidly situated right on the banks of the Bosphorus. Exhibits to look out for, on the main floor, are lavishly adorned imperial caïques – high-prowed barges that were used for ferrying the royal family along the Bosphorus. The largest, built for Sultan Mehmet IV in 1648, was 40-m- (130-ft-) long and required 144 *bostancıs* (oarsmen) to row it. Beautifully carved figureheads of ships along with a chronological display of the Ottoman naval history are housed on the floor below.

### ④ Yıldız Palace
(Yıldız Sarayı)

MAP C4 ■ Yıldız Cad, Beşiktaş ■ (0212) 258 30 80 ■ Palace open 9am–6pm Wed–Mon; park open 10am–5:30pm daily (till 4pm in winter) ■ Adm charge for palace

Much of this rambling palace was built by Sultan Abdül Hamit II (ruled 1876–1909), a highly skilled carpenter whose former workshop now houses the Yıldız Palace Museum. The park and its pavilions are also open to the public. In the grounds is the Imperial Porcelain Factory, now mass-producing china where once they made fine porcelain.

Yıldız Palace in Beşiktaş

**Bosphorus Bridge**

inlaid stairs in the Fountain Room, the hand-decorated doorknobs, the Bohemian crystal chandeliers, the Hereke carpets and the walnut-and-rosewood furniture made by Abdül Hamit himself (see also p91).

### 7 Aşiyan Museum
(Aşiyan Müzesi)
MAP U2 ■ Aşiyan Yokuşu, Bebek ■ (0212) 263 69 86 ■ Open 9am–4:30pm Tue, Wed, Fri, Sat

The poet and utopian philosopher Tevfik Fikret (1867–1915), founder of the Edebiyat-i Cedid (New Literature) movement, built this wooden mansion, now on the campus of Boğaziçi University, in 1906. It recalls the movement with the personal belongings and photos of the members.

### 5 Bosphorus Bridge
(Boğaziçi Köprüsü)
MAP C4

In 1973, to mark the 50th anniversary of the establishment of the Republic of Turkey, this soaring creation, linking Europe and Asia across the Bosphorus straits, was officially opened. At 1,560 m (5,120 ft) long, it is the world's sixth-longest suspension bridge. Pedestrians are not allowed onto the bridge, so if you want plenty of time to admire the view, cross at rush hour when the heavy traffic routinely becomes gridlocked.

### 6 Beylerbeyi Palace
(Beylerbeyi Sarayi)
MAP C5 ■ Çayırbaşı Cad (next to Bosphorus Bridge) ■ (0216) 321 93 20 ■ Bus 15 from Üsküdar ■ Open 9am–5pm (to 4pm Oct–Apr) Tue, Wed, Fri–Sun (guided tours only) ■ Adm charge

This small, frivolously ornate powder-puff of a palace was built in 1860–65 by Sultan Abdül Aziz as a summer retreat. It was here that Sultan Abdül Hamit II lived out his days in captivity after he was deposed in 1909. You will either be charmed or overwhelmed by the incredible detailing of architect Sarkis Balyan's Oriental Rococo style. Look for the

### 8 Fortress of Europe
(Rumeli Hisarı)
MAP U2 ■ Yahya Kemal Cad ■ (0212) 263 53 05 ■ Open 9am–4:30pm Thu–Tue ■ Adm charge

In 1452, as he prepared for his final attack on Constantinople, Mehmet II built this vast fortress at the narrowest point of the Bosphorus, opposite the earlier Fortress of Asia (Anadolu Hisarı) (see p94), to cut the

---

#### PRINCELY PARANOIA

Terrified both of plots to seize his throne and of seaborne attack by foreign warships on Dolmabahçe Palace, Sultan Abdül Hamit II (ruled 1876–1909; below) removed himself from the Dolmabahçe to live at the much smaller Yıldız Palace (see p91), the core of which – the State Apartments (Büyük Mabeyn) – dates to the reign of Sultan Selim III (ruled 1789–1807). Abdül Hamit built a sprawling complex of pavilions and villas in the palace grounds, and he supposedly never spent two nights in the same bed. He was over-thrown in April 1909.

flow of supplies reaching the city. The castle's three main towers are surrounded by a huge curtain wall with 13 bastions. The main tower later became a prison.

**Fortress of Europe**

**⑨ Sakıp Sabancı Museum**
(Sakıp Sabancı Müzesi)
MAP U2 ▪ Sakıp Sabancı Cad 42, Emirgan ▪ (0212) 277 22 00 ▪ Open 10am–6pm Tue–Sun (to 8pm Wed) ▪ Adm charge

The summer residence of the Sabancı family of industrialists from 1951 to 1999, the Atlı Köşk (Horse Mansion) is now a museum set in stunning gardens that overlook the Bosphorus. The exhibits here include calligraphy of the Ottoman era, and paintings by leading 19th- and 20th-century Turkish artists. The modern extension is a well-designed art gallery housing major touring exhibitions.

**⑩ Sadberk Hanım Museum**
(Sadberk Hanım Müzesi)
MAP U1 ▪ Piyasa Cad 27–29, Büyükdere ▪ (0212) 242 38 13 ▪ Open 10am–5pm Thu–Tue ▪ Adm charge ▪ www.sadberkhanimmuzesi.org.tr

The Sadberk Hanım Museum boasts a must-see collection that includes a range of Turkish embroidery as well as Anatolian figurines, Assyrian cuneiform trade tablets, Hittite coins and gold jewellery.

**Anatolian figurine**

**A WALK THROUGH KARAKÖY**

▶ **MORNING**

Start your day at the Karaköy tram stop, then head uphill to the early 20th-century Minerva Han, adorned with cupid statues on its tiled façade. Turn left along **Voyvoda Caddesi**, named for Vlad the Impaler, whose decapitated head (it is said) was displayed here. If you have time, explore the art gallery, **SALT Galata** and the **Ottoman Bank Museum**. The **Kamondo Steps** lead towards the Galata Tower. Walk back down along Karaköy Caddesi and turn right to visit **Yeraltı Camii**, an underground mosque built on the site of an old Byzantine tower.

**AFTERNOON**

Continue along Karaköy and turn left onto Rihtim Caddesi. The **Güllüoğlu** baklava shop here is the finest in Turkey, with pastries sold by the kilo; the Galata Rihtim Köftecisi nearby offers a healthier option for lunch. Follow the road round between two fine small mosques, the **Nusretiye Mosque** (on the right), built by Kirkor Balyan in the 1820s, and the **Kılıç Ali Paşa Mosque**, built by Sinan in 1580 and named after a famous admiral in Süleyman I's navy. Turn right onto the main road and, just after the Mimar Sinan University building, turn right again. Follow the signs through the old docks area to **Istanbul Modern** (see p91), where you can watch the sunset with a cocktail in the chic café-bar overlooking the Bosphorus. Then take the tram to Kabataş and the funicular up the hill to Taksim Square (see p84) for an evening meal.

See map on p90

# The Best of the Rest

### ① National Palaces Painting Museum
(Milli Saraylar Resim Müzesi)

MAP C5 ■ Hayrettin Paşa Iskelesi Sok, Beşiktaş ■ (0212) 261 42 98 ■ Bus 25E, 28, 40, 56 ■ Open 9am–5pm Tue, Wed, Fri–Sun

Fine art from the 19th and 20th centuries is displayed in this museum, in the Crown Princes' Suite at Dolmabahçe Palace.

### ② Çırağan Palace
(Çırağan Sarayı)

MAP C5 ■ Çırağan Cad 32, Beşiktaş ■ (0212) 326 46 46 ■ Bus 25E, 40 ■ www.ciragan-palace.com

Sultan Abdül Aziz spent a fortune on this confection of a palace, built in 1874, before pronouncing it damp and moving out. The Palace is now home to a luxury hotel.

### ③ Ortaköy

MAP C4 ■ Bus 25RE, 40

This pretty village beside the Bosphorus Bridge has many waterfront cafés, restaurants and clubs, and a weekend craft market.

### ④ Arnavutköy

MAP U3 ■ Ferry or road

Once noted for its strawberries, the village of Arnavutköy is now better known for the charming *yalıs* (wooden mansions) that line its pretty waterfront.

**Waterfront, Arnavutköy**

### ⑤ Automobile Museum
(SAV Otomobil Müzesi)

MAP V3 ■ Bosna Bulvarı 104, Çengelköy (Asian side) ■ (0216) 329 50 30 ■ Open Fri–Sun ■ Adm charge

Here you will find Turkey's largest collection of antique cars.

### ⑥ Küçüksu Palace
(Küçüksu Kasrı)

MAP U3 ■ Küçüksu Cad, Beykoz (Asian side) ■ (0216) 332 33 03 ■ Bus 15 from Üsküdar ■ Open 9:30am–4pm Tue, Wed, Fri–Sun (guided tours only) ■ Adm charge

Küçüksu, with two rivers known to the Ottomans as the "Sweet Waters of Asia", was a playground for the Imperial court. The palace was built as a hunting lodge in 1857 for Abdül Mecit.

### ⑦ Fortress of Asia
(Anadolu Hisarı)

MAP U2 ■ Boat or road to Kanlıca

Built by Beyazıt I in 1391, this fortress on the Asian side is a smaller counterpart to the Fortress of Europe, added by Mehmet II in 1452, directly across the Bosphorus (see p92–3).

### ⑧ Emirgan Park
(Emirgan Parkı)

MAP U2 ■ Emirgan Sahil Yolu ■ Bus 25E, 40 ■ Open 7am–10pm daily

This attractive park with botanic planting is one venue for the Tulip Festival each April (see p47 & p56).

### ⑨ Borusan Contemporary

MAP U2 ■ Perili Köşk Baltalımanı Hısar Cad 5, Rumelihisarı ■ (0212) 393 52 00 ■ Bus 22, 40T ■ Open 10am–8pm Sat & Sun ■ Adm charge

A fashionable office block in the week, Istanbul's coolest gallery at weekends, with great Bosphorus views from the roof terrace.

### ⑩ Anadolu Kavağı

MAP V1 ■ Asian side

This is the last stop for the Bosphorus ferry. Climb the hill to Yoros Castle, a ruined 14th-century Genoese fortress.

# Bars, Cafés and Restaurants

**PRICE CATEGORIES**

For a typical meal of *meze* and main
course for one without alcohol, and
including taxes and extra charges.

₺ under ₺45  ₺₺ ₺45–90  ₺₺₺ over ₺90

**1 Muzedechanga**
MAP U2 ▪ Sakıp Sabancı Cad 22,
Emirgan ▪ (0212) 323 09 01 ▪ ₺₺₺
This hip eating place adjoins the Sakıp
Sabancı Museum *(see p93)*. Its cool
Scandanavian style complements the
sophisticated fusion cuisine on offer.

**2 Feriye Lokantası**
MAP C4 ▪ Çırağan Cad 40,
Ortaköy ▪ (0212) 227 22 16/7 ▪ ₺₺
Picturesquely situated on the
Ortaköy waterfront, the Feriye serves
delicious Ottoman dishes including
charcoal-grilled lamb. Book ahead.

**3 The House Café**
MAP C4 ▪ Salhane Sok 1,
Ortaköy ▪ (0212) 227 26 99
▪ Book for brunch ▪ ₺₺
The Ortaköy branch of this popular
café chain serves unusual pizzas
(like pear, Roquefort and honey),
together with seafood, and brunch
staples. Its waterfront decking is a
draw during the summer months.

**4 Anjelique**
MAP C4 ▪ Muallim Naci
Cad, Salhane Sok 5, Ortaköy
▪ (0212) 327 28 44/5 ▪ ₺₺
On the first-floor waterfront terrace
is the upmarket Da Mario Italian
restaurant (summer only), while
the second and third floors serve
international cuisine. The two upper
floors become a nightclub after the
dishes are cleared away.

**5 Kıyı**
MAP U2 ▪ Kefelıköy Cad 126,
Tarabya ▪ (0212) 262 00 02
A smart and stylish fish joint in the
posh suburb of Tarabya. The decor
is plain chic and the *meze* and fish
mains are cooked to perfection.

Laledan, Beşiktaş

**6 Laledan, Beşiktaş**
MAP C5 ▪ Çırağan Cad,
Beşiktaş ▪ (0212) 236 73 33 ▪ ₺₺₺
Part of the luxurious Çırağan
Palace Hotel Kempinski, the
Laledan restaurant serves great
brunches in a fairy-tale setting.

**7 Supperclub**
MAP C4 ▪ Muallim Naci Cad
65, Ortaköy ▪ (0212) 261 19 88
This trendy club on the Bosphorus
waterfront is an ambitious and
intriguing concept. There's a cool,
all-white interior, subtle electronic
sounds and plenty of lounging
sofas to chill out on.

**8 Poseidon**
MAP U3 ▪ Çevdet Paşa
Cad 58 ▪ (0212) 287 95 31 ▪ ₺₺
Located in trendy Bebek, this
chic seafood restaurant offers
mouthwatering food.

**9 Reina**
MAP C4 ▪ Muallim Naci Cad 44,
Ortaköy ▪ (0212) 259 59 19 ▪ Adm
charge Fri, Sat; free at other times
Dance the night away to European
club sounds at this unashamedly
pretentious nightspot.

**10 Suna'nın Yeri**
MAP U3 ▪ İskele Cad 2/A,
Kandilli ▪ (0216) 332 32 41 ▪ ₺₺
An unpretentious and well-
established fish joint by the ferry
dock in the Asian suburb of Kandilli.
The food here is a fraction of the
price of most Bosphorus fish
restaurants, and just as good.

See map on p90

# TOP 10 Asian Istanbul and Princes' Islands

Asian Istanbul is just a 20-minute ferry ride across the Bosphorus or one metro stop through the Bosphorus tunnel. Üsküdar is home to some venerable Ottoman mosques and the quirky off-shore Leander's Tower. To the south, Kadıköy is more lively than conservative Üsküdar, with plenty of bars. Between these two suburbs are the Florence Nightingale Museum and German-built Haydarpaşa Station. The Princes' Islands are easily reached by ferry from Kabataş. Places of exile in the Byzantine era, summer retreats for minority Jewish and Christian groups in the 19th century, today they are traffic-free and an ideal place to swim, cycle or just relax at a harbour front restaurant.

## AREA MAP OF ASIAN ISTANBUL AND PRINCES' ISLANDS

**Leander's Tower**

### 1 Leander's Tower
(Kız Kulesi)

MAP W3 ▪ (0216) 342 47 47
▪ Tower open 12:30–6:30pm
Mon–Fri, 9:15am–6:30pm Sat
& Sun; restaurant open to 1am

According to Greek myth, Leander
drowned while trying to swim the
Dardanelles from his home town
of Abydos on the Asian side to
meet his lover Hero, a priestess
in Sestos on the other shore. He is
commemorated in the English name
for this 18th-century tower on an
islet offshore from Üsküdar. Its
Turkish name means "Maiden's
Tower", in reference to a legendary
Byzantine princess who was told that
she would die of a snakebite and was
locked up on the island for her own
protection, only for a
snake to arrive in a basket
of figs. In its time, the
tower has served as a
quarantine centre and a
customs office; nowadays,
it houses a restaurant. It
had a cameo role in the
1999 James Bond film
*The World Is Not Enough*.

### 2 İskele Mosque
(İskele Camii)

MAP X2 ▪ Kurşunlu Medrese Sok
▪ (0216) 321 93 20 ▪ Ferry Üsküdar
or Marmaray ▪ Open daily (closed at
prayer times)

This beautiful mosque, officially
called the Mihrimah Sultan Mosque,
was a present, built in 1547–8, from
Süleyman I to his favourite daughter,
Mihrimah. Its raised
portico offers fine views
down to the main square.

### 3 Şemsi Paşa Mosque
(Şemsi Paşa Camii)

MAP W2 ▪ Sahil Yolu
▪ Ferry Üsküdar
▪ Open daily

Legend has it that birds
will not land on or dirty
this mosque out of
respect for its beauty
and the reputation of its architect. It
is one of Mimar Sinan's last works
*(see p27)*, built in 1580 for Şemsi
Ahmet Paşa, Grand Vizier to
Süleyman I. Made of white stone,
it is very modest in size and sits
in a picturesque location among
the waterfront fish restaurants.

### 4 Florence Nightingale Museum

MAP X5 ▪ Selimiye Kışlası, Çeşme-i-
Kebir Cad ▪ (0216) 556 81 66 ▪ Ferry
to Harem ▪ Open 9am–5pm Mon–Fri
▪ Visitors should fax (0216) 553 10 09
requesting permission to visit, at
least 2 days in advance, giving names,
nationalities, passport details and
contact number

In the northwest tower of the Selimiye
Barracks is a moving tribute to the
formidable Englishwoman
Florence Nightingale
(1820–1910), who in 1854
gathered a group of 38
women and set up a
hospital in Istanbul to
nurse thousands of
Turkish and allied soldiers
wounded during the
Crimean War – inventing
modern nursing practice
along the way. The

**The Lady with the Lamp, 1891**

museum contains her photographs
and medallions, gifts from Sultan
Abdül Mecit, and the lamp from which
she got her nickname, "the Lady of
the Lamp". The vast barracks in
which the museum is situated
were begun in 1828 by Mahmut II
to replace an earlier military building
constucted by Selim III.

**Interior of Haydarpaşa Station**

neighbourhood feel. The lively market area by the docks has fresh fruit and vegetables galore and is a good place to stock up on provisions. A nostalgic tram rumbles through the area down to fashionable Moda, in Asian Istanbul, where you can enjoy a pleasant seafront stroll. Fenerbahçe – one of Turkey's top football clubs – has its grounds, Şükrü Saraçoğlu Stadium, close by, so watch out for traffic jams on match days.

### 5 Haydarpaşa Station
MAP C6 ■ Haydarpaşa İstasyon Cad ■ (0216) 336 04 75 ■ Ferry to Haydarpaşa or Kadıköy

Haydarpaşa Station is the largest station in Turkey and the most westerly train stop in Asia. It was completed in 1908 by German architects Otto Ritter and Helmuth Cuno, a gift from the German government of Kaiser Wilhelm II. Until recently, the station was the departure point for travellers heading further into Anatolia; trains to Europe depart from Sirkeci Station (see p62). Now that the Marmaray tunnel under the Bosphorus has been completed, the fate of both stations is undecided.

### 6 Kadıköy
MAP C6 ■ Frequent ferries from Eminönü

Kadıköy, first settled as long ago as the Neolithic era, was the site of the Greek colony of Chalcedon, founded in 676 BC, nine years before the establishment of Byzantion (see p60). However, Chalcedon proved to be more vulnerable to invaders than Byzantion, and it failed to flourish. Today, Kadıköy is a popular and attractive shopping area, but it has maintained its cosy,

### 7 Kınalıada
MAP V6 ■ Ferry from Kabataş

"Henna Island", Kınalıada is the nearest island to the city but the least visited. It has some reasonable beaches, and is popular in summer with Istanbul's dwindling Armenian community, which has a pretty church just above the village.

**The main settlement on Kınalıada**

### 8 Burgazada
MAP U6 ■ Ferry from Kabataş

Beyond Kınalıada, the attractive little island of Burgazada is topped by a badly ruined Byzantine monastery. Of interest here is the museum of bohemian Turkish writer Sait Faik, which occupies a delightful period house (see p100). Aside from this, visitors usually content themselves with a horse and carriage ride, a splash in the sea, or a fish meal along the waterfront.

**Taking a ride on Heybeliada**

### 9 Heybeliada
MAP V6 ■ Ferry from Kabataş

"Saddlebag Island" is so called as the island comprises two green hills, with a saddle between them. The third island in the chain, it's an ideal place to hire a bike and cycle around or ride on a horse-drawn carriage. The Greek Orthodox Haghia Triada seminary (see p100) dominates one hilltop. There are several pay beaches dotted around the island.

### 10 Büyükada
MAP V6 ■ Ferry from Kabataş

"Big Island" is, unsurprisingly, the largest of the islands, and the furthest from Istanbul. Horse and carriage rides are big here, as is the steep walk up to the Monastery of St George (see p100) and the next-door restaurant – both with fine sea views. Hire a bike and cycle to the Museum of the Princes' Islands (see p100).

#### THE MARMARAY

The name Marmaray comes from combining the name of the Sea of Marmara, with ray, the Turkish word for "rail". In 2013, a section of one of Turkey's most significant infrastructure projects went into service when the tunnel from Sirkeci to Üsküdar opened. The Marmaray tunnel will be the central point of a revamped railway network running all the way from Halkali on the European side of the city to Gebze on the Asian side, greatly speeding up transport around town. The Third Bosphorus Bridge is set for completion in 2016.

### A DAY IN ASIA

#### MORNING

Take the tram to Kabataş. Make sure you have your Istanbulkart or buy a handful of tokens at the ferry terminal. Pick up a timetable to keep an eye on ferry times. Summer weekends are very crowded aboard, so arrive early to bag a seat on a Kınalıada-bound ferry (the journey takes around 50 minutes). Visit the small **Armenian chapel** on a hill just above Kınalıada's main settlement before catching another ferry south to **Burgazada**. Either hire a bike or horse-drawn carriage (fayton in Turkish) and head around the coast to **Kalpazankaya** (see p101) to enjoy a fine fish meal at the well-regarded restaurant here. It overlooks a small beach where you can swim in season.

#### AFTERNOON

Ride the ferry onto **Heybeliada** and explore the harbour front area. Look out for the **Aya Nikola** Greek Orthodox Church and have a Turkish coffee on the seafront while waiting for a ferry onto **Büyükada**. To find out about the history of these islands, either hire a bike or fayton and head for the **Museum of the Princes' Islands** (see p100) on Büyükada's east coast. The best (albeit stony) beach is **Halik Köyü**, on the west coast. Alternatively explore the fin de siècle mansions (Trotsky lived in one from 1929 to 1933) dotted around the town, or walk up to the **Monastery of St George** (see p100). The sea bus back to Kabataş takes half an hour; ferries, over an hour.

*See map on p96*

# The Best of the Rest

### 1 Yeni Valide Mosque
(Yeni Valide Camii)
MAP X2 ■ Hakimiyeti Milliye Cad ■ Ferry Üsküdar or Marmaray ■ Open daily

This imposing mosque was built in 1710 by Ahmet III for his mother, Gülnuş Emetullah.

### 2 Atik Valide Mosque
(Atik Valide Camii)
MAP Y3 ■ Çinili Cami Sok ■ Bus 12C from Üsküdar ■ Open prayer times only

The huge complex of the Old Mosque of the Sultan's Mother was completed in 1583 for Nurbanu Valide Sultan, the Venetian-born Jewish wife of Selim II.

### 3 Tiled Mosque
(Çinili Camii)
MAP C5 ■ Çinili Hamam Sok 1, Üsküdar ■ Ferry or Marmaray to Üsküdar, then 20-min walk ■ Open prayer times only

Don't miss the İznik tiles inside this mosque, built in 1640.

### 4 British Crimean War Cemetery
MAP C6 ■ Off Burhan Felek Cad ■ Ferry Harem then 15-min walk

Most of the 6,000 Crimean War soldiers in this cemetery died of cholera rather than in battle. The War Memorial was erected in 1857.

### 5 Istanbul Toy Museum
(Istanbul Oyuncak Müzesi)
MAP U4 ■ Ömerpaşa Cad, Dr Zeki Zeren Sok 17, Göztepe ■ (0216) 359 45 50/1 ■ Open 9:30am–6pm Tue–Sun ■ Adm charge

Highlights of this collection of toys and miniatures from around the world include a French miniature violin from 1817 and a US doll from the 1820s.

### 6 Kuzguncuk
MAP C5

Wander through the streets of wooden houses in this old Jewish quarter, then stop for refreshment in one of the many eateries on the main street, İcadiye Caddesi.

### 7 Sait Faik Museum
(Sait Faik Müzesi)
MAP U6 ■ Cayiri Sok 15, Burgazada ■ Open 10am–noon & 2–5pm Tue–Sun, 10am–noon Sat

Turkey's answer to Mark Twain lived in this beautifully preserved home.

### 8 Haghia Triada Monastery
(Aya Triada Manastırı)
MAP V6 ■ Aya Triada Manastiriş, Heybeliada ■ (0216) 351 85 63

The Turkish authorities controversially closed the seminary here in the 1970s. Today it still functions as a monastery, but you need to book to gain entry.

### 9 Museum of the Princes' Islands (Adalar Müzesi)
MAP V6 ■ Aya Nikola Mevkii, Büyükada ■ (0216) 382 64 30 ■ Open 9am–6pm Tue–Sun ■ Adm charge

The focus here is on period photographs of the Christian communities who lived here in the 19th century.

### 10 Monastery of St George
(Aya Yorgi Manastır)
MAP V6 ■ Yuca Tepe, Büyükada ■ Open 9am–6pm daily

Situated on one of the islands' two hills, this working Orthodox monastery dates to the 12th century.

**Monastery of St George**

# Bars, Cafés and Restaurants

**PRICE CATEGORIES**

For a typical meal of *meze* and main course for one without alcohol, and including taxes and extra charges.

₺ under ₺45 ₺₺ ₺45–90 ₺₺₺ over ₺90

Çiya restaurant

### 1 Kanaat, Üskudar
MAP X2 ▪ Selmanipak Cad 9 ▪ (0216) 553 37 91 ▪ ₺

This traditional *lokanta* is as popular today as when it opened in 1933. It offers inexpensive but excellent Turkish food, as well as deliciously tempting puddings.

### 2 Otantik Anadolu Yemekleri, Kadıköy
MAP C6 ▪ Muvakkithane Cad 62–4 ▪ (0216) 330 71 44 ▪ ₺

Otantik offers no-frills, hearty Anatolian cuisine with *gözleme* (stuffed crepes), fresh chicken, lamb casseroles and stuffed cabbage leaves.

### 3 Kadife Sokak, Kadıköy
MAP C6

Known to locals simply as Barlar Sokak ("Bar Street"), this lane is bursting with bars, cafés and clubs catering mainly to the young. Listen to avant-garde jazz or electronica in Karga (No. 16), taste fine wines in the garden at Isis (No. 26), or sit back and chill in Arka Oda (No. 18).

### 4 Buddha Rock Bar, Kadıköy
MAP U5 ▪ Caferağa Mah, Kadife Sok 14 ▪ (0216) 345 87 98 ▪ ₺

This is a popular student bar, offering a range of cheap drinks, an energetic crowd, and live rock and blues alternating with a DJ.

### 5 Tarihi Moda İskelesi, Moda
MAP U4 ▪ At the far end of the pier, off Moda İskele Cad ▪ ₺₺

In an ornate little building on the old quayside, this café serves decent food and is a perfect spot for lunch.

### 6 Çiya, Kadıköy
MAP C6 ▪ Caferağa Mah, Guneşlibahçe Sok 44 ▪ (0216) 418 51 15 ▪ ₺₺

The kebabs in this informal gourmet restaurant are wonderful – the salads and *meze* are worth a look, too. There's a nice roof terrace.

### 7 Kalpazankaya, Burgazada
MAP U6 ▪ Kalpazankaya Mevkii ▪ (0216) 381 11 11 ▪ ₺₺

A relaxed place on Burgazada's west shore with hot and cold *meze* and delicious grilled fish.

### 8 Deniz Yıldızı, Kadıköy
MAP U5 ▪ İskele Cad, Eski Kadıköy İskelesi ▪ (0216) 349 95 17 ▪ ₺₺

Watch the boats from this old restaurant-bar on the seafront. Open all day serving sandwiches, salads, beer, coffee and full restaurant menu.

### 9 Viktor Levi, Kadıköy
MAP C6 ▪ Moda Cad, Damacı Sok 4, Kadıköy ▪ (0216) 449 93 29 ▪ ₺₺

Popular wine bar in the heart of Kadıköy, with a delightful garden. Offers a wide range of sumptuous meals for lunch and dinner.

### 10 Kır Gazinosu, Büyükada
MAP V6 ▪ Kır Gazinosu, Aya Yorgi, Yüce Tepe ▪ ₺₺

Next to the Monastery of St George on Yüce Tepe hill, this casual place serves excellent starters, savoury pastries, chips and grills.

*See map on p96*

# Streetsmart

Colourful buildings lining
Yerebatan Caddesi in Sultanahmet

# Getting To and Around Istanbul

## Arriving by Air

The city of Istanbul has two main airports, **Atatürk International** and Sabiha Gökçen, with a third major international airport set to open in 2018. Flight times from London are 3.5 hours and from New York 9 hours.

Atatürk International, Istanbul's principal airport, is located on the European side of the city, 24 km (15 miles) west of the centre. **Havataş** shuttle buses run every half an hour between 4am and 1am to Aksaray (for Sultanahmet and the Old City), then on to Taksim (for Galata and Beyoğlu); journey time is between 40 minutes and 1 hour. The M1 metro also runs to the city centre; change at Zeytinburnu to the T1 tram for Sultanahmet/ Old City. For Galata or Beyoğlu, take the M1 metro to Yenikapı, then the M2 metro to either Şişhane or Taksim. Both the metro and the tram service run approximately 6am–midnight daily, taking around the same time as the shuttle bus. Taking a taxi from the airport should cost around ₺70.

The smaller Sabiha Gökçen Airport is used mainly by European budget carriers, such as easyJet, and is located on the Asian side of Istanbul, some 50 km (30 miles) from the city centre. Havataş shuttle buses run to Taksim Square half-hourly between 4am and 1am, taking a minimum of 1 hour. A taxi will cost around ₺90.

## Arriving by Coach

Turkish-operated coaches arrive from several European cities, including Berlin, Prague, Vienna and Sofia. For services from London contact **Eurolines**. Istanbul's main coach station is **Esenler**, 10 km (6 miles) northwest of the city centre, where services from Europe terminate. Esenler is also the main terminus for domestic services, though some stop at **Harem**, on the Asian shore. Many bus companies offer courtesy buses into the city centre; the alternative is the M1 metro.

## Arriving by Rail

Owing to huge transport infrastructure projects in Istanbul, reaching the city by train from Europe is difficult. At the time of writing the only train from Europe, the Bosphorus Express from Bucharest, was terminating at the Bulgarian–Turkish border, with onward travel by bus. **Man in Seat 61** is a useful website for booking train seats across Europe.

## Arrival by Sea

Istanbul is a major cruise ship destination, with ships docking at the confluence of the Golden Horn and Bosphorus right in the heart of the city.

## Travelling by Metro and Tram

The cheapest and most convenient way to travel around the city is by a combination of metro and tram, especially if you use an Istanbulkart. Both systems operate between 6am and midnight, but can be very crowded during peak periods.

The M1 line links the Old City with Atatürk Airport, and the M2 line the Old City with Galata, Beyoğlu and Taksim via a bridge across the Golden Horn. The Marmaray line, opened in 2013, runs west from Sirkeci station to Kazlıçesme, on the line of the Theodosian Walls, and east under the Bosphorus Strait to Üsküdar in Asia.

The tram route of most interest to visitors is the T1 between Bağcılar and Kabataş, which links the Old City and Sultanahmet with the shopping, gallery and nightlife districts across the Golden Horn in Galata and Beyoğlu. The T1 tram links in with the metro system at Zeytinburnu (for Atatürk Airport), Karaköy (for the Tünel funicular) and Kabataş (for the funicular to Taksim Square and ferry terminal for the Princes' Islands). A period tram runs up and down Istiklal Caddesi between Tünel and Taksim Square.

## Travelling by Funicular

The Tünel, connecting Karaköy to İstiklal Caddesi, the city's main shopping and entertainment street, is one of the world's oldest undergrounds (see p86). A second funicular runs from the Bosphorus shore at Kabataş to Taksim Square.

## Travelling by Bus

**Municipal buses** are often crowded, the drivers usually only speak Turkish and the schedules are unreliable. Sometimes, however, they are the only public transport available – running up the European or Asian shores of the Bosphorus, for example – so some visitors may want to make the effort to use them.

## Travelling by Ferry

Travelling around Istanbul's waterways by ferry is a pleasure. The main dock at Eminönü has departures to the Asian suburbs of Üsküdar and Kadıköy, and up the Golden Horn. It is also the departure point for Bosphorus cruise excursions (see pp34–5). Ferries for Asia also depart from Karaköy and those for the Princes' Islands from Kabataş. Ferries are run by **City Lines** (Şehir Hatları), while faster sea buses to the Princes' Islands are operated by **Istanbul Sea Buses** (İDO).

## Tickets

Buy tokens for buses, the metro, tram and ferries from kiosks near stations and stops. Alternatively the Istanbulkart travel smart card can be used on all of these and saves around 25 per cent per journey. As you enter the form of transport, touch the reader with your card; recharge the card when necessary. The card deposit is ₺6; load credit from kiosks, stations or vending machines.

## Travelling by Taxi

A licensed taxi (taksi) is yellow in colour and shows a light on top when it is available for hire. Before you set off, always check that the meter is switched on. Better still, agree the fare with your driver before you get in. Day and night rides are charged at the same rate. Beware of drivers taking the long way around in order to short-change you.

## Dolmuş

These shared minibuses run along set routes, and only depart when they are full. They will pick up or set down where you want along the route. Ranks have a blue sign with a black D on a white background. Several useful dolmuş services leave from around Taksim Square. They are a cheap form of transport, but can make for a slow journey.

## By Car

Driving in the city centre is a nightmare. The larger business hotels have parking, most in the Old City do not. Hire a car and driver to see sights that are further apart.

## On Foot

Walking is the most rewarding way to see most parts of the city, especially the historic core bounded by the Theodosian Walls. Unfortunately streets are often unmarked, so it's easy to wander off track. Pavements are often rough and uneven, and kerbs high, so wear decent shoes or boots. Traffic only stops at light-controlled crossings.

## Tours

There are plenty of tours on offer, by bus, car or on foot (see p111). Trips to sights such as Gallipoli and Troy, Edirne or Bursa are also available.

(see pp34–5)

(see p111)

## DIRECTORY

### AIRPORTS

**Atatürk International**
Yeşilköy (European side)
( (0212) 444 98 28
w ataturkairport.com

### COACHES

**Esenler Bus Terminal**
( (0212) 658 05 05

**Eurolines**
( UK: 08717 818181
w eurolines.com

**Harem Bus Terminal**
( (0216) 333 37 63

### TRAINS

**Man in Seat 61**
w maninseat61.com

### METRO AND TRAM

**Istanbul Ulaşım**
( (0212) 444 00 88
w istanbul-ulasim.com.tr

**Istanbulkart**
w istanbulkart.iett.
gov.tr

### BUSES

**Havataş**
( (0212) 444 26 56
w havatas.com

**Municipal buses**
( (0212) 372 22 22
w iett.gov.tr

### FERRIES

**City Lines**
( (0212) 444 18 51
w sehirhatlari.com.tr

**Istanbul Sea Buses**
( 0850 222 4436
w ido.com.tr

# Practical Information

## Passports and Visas

To enter Turkey, you need a full passport valid for at least six months. Most people requiring a visa must apply in advance online. The cost varies depending on your nationality: UK ($20), Canada ($60), Australia ($60), USA ($20) and Ireland ($20). Payment can be made by debit or credit card.

A multiple-entry tourist visa valid for up to 90 days in 180 days will be issued. South Africans or people with British National Overseas passports must apply for a visa at a consulate before travelling. New Zealand nationals receive a free tourist visa on arrival that is valid for up to three months. Entry requirements can change so check with the **Turkish Ministry of Foreign Affairs** for the latest information.

## Customs Regulations and Immigration

Visitors may bring 50 cigars, 600 cigarettes, 200 g tobacco, 1 litre spirits, 2 litres wine, 2 kg tea, coffee and chocolate, 600 ml perfume and unlimited currency. Penalties for possessing narcotics are very harsh.

## Travel Safety Advice

Visitors can get up-to-date safety information from the UK **Foreign and Commonwealth Office**, the **State Department** in the US and the **Department of Foreign Affairs and Trade** in Australia.

## Travel Insurance

You are strongly advised to take out travel insurance with full medical cover, including repatriation by air. If buying a Europe-only policy, check that it will also cover you on the Asian side of Istanbul.

## Health

Before travelling to Istanbul, make sure your basic inoculations are up-to-date, and check with your doctor about Hepatitis A and Hepatitis B vaccinations.

Rabies is prevalent in Turkey, so be wary of the city's numerous stray dogs and cats. Mosquitoes can be a problem in summer, so take some repellent. While Istanbul tap water is considered safe, it is advisable to drink bottled water. If you are vulnerable to stomach upsets, foods to avoid include salad and seafood from street stalls. See the Directory opposite for emergency services telephone numbers.

There are numerous pharmacies *(eczane)* across the city. Duty *(nobetçi)* chemists, often stationed near hospitals, are open all night. The state hospital system is fine in an emergency, but private hospitals are more efficient, and are less expensive than in many parts of the world. Well-regarded hospitals conveniently located for most visitors include the **Amerikan Hastanesi** (American Hospital),

the **Alman Hastanesi** (German Hospital), **Cerrahpaşa Hastanesi** and **Sen Jorj Avustrya Hastanesi** (St George's Austrian Hospital).

Turkish dentists are well-trained and many have the latest equipment. Fees are relatively low and some visitors come to Istanbul just to have their teeth fixed. **Prodent-Can Ergene** and **Reha Sezgin** are recommended clinics.

## Personal Security

Istanbul has a fairly low crime rate, but take the normal precautions against pickpockets, particularly on the crowded public transport system and busy shopping areas. Districts with bad reputations include Tarlabaşı, near Taksim Square, where prostitution (straight, gay and transgender) and petty theft are a problem, and the line of the Theodosian Walls, where vagrants and alcoholics may be a nuisance towards dusk. Lone male visitors should beware of confidence tricksters in nightclubs, especially those around Taksim Square, who trick the unwary into buying hugely expensive drinks for attractive females. The spiking of drinks is not unknown, either.

Terrorism is a potential threat, with al-Qaeda hitting the British Consulate, HSBC bank and synagogues in 2003. Protests often escalate quickly into violence, as with the Gezi Park (part of Taksim Square) riots of

2013. Marches often take place along İstiklal Caddesi and up to Taksim Square and are tightly controlled by riot police with batons, shields, helmets and teargas. Since the civil war started in 2011, Syrian refugees have become a common sight on Istanbul's streets.

Do not joke, make light of or criticize Turkey, its founding father, Atatürk, or the country's flag, as the vast majority of Turks are very nationalistic and will take offence. Defacing a banknote (invariably adorned with an image of Atatürk) or the flag is a criminal offence.

Turkey has become more conservative in recent years, with head-scarved women a common sight, and restrictions on visiting mosques for non-Muslims more obvious. Couples should beware of displaying affection in public, and never make jokes about Islam.

Many younger Turkish women, particularly Istanbulites, dress much as they would anywhere else in Europe, and tight jeans, singlets and fairly short skirts are common-place. Foreign women out for the night in areas like Beyoğlu often do likewise. However, such dress is not appropriate in many parts of the city, or when visiting mosques. Women travelling alone should be extra-careful; dress conservatively, don't make eye contact with males and avoid backstreets, especially at night. If you are being harassed, make a scene and someone should come to your aid. The Turkish police are usually polite and helpful.

In tourist areas, report losses, theft or other problems to the **Tourist Police** – translators are generally present 9am–5pm Monday to Friday. If you get into trouble, most countries have consulates in Istanbul – they will assist with missing documents, arrange repatriation, or help you to find legal representation if needed. It is illegal to be out in public without photo ID; photocopy the relevant page of your passport and carry that with you for security.

Istanbul is in a major earthquake zone and the last serious quake to take place was in 1999. As a result, building rules and regulations were tightened up, but still today many of the city's structures – especially older ones – are not adequately quakeproofed.

## DIRECTORY

### PASSPORTS AND VISAS
**Online visas**
w evisa.gov.tr
**Turkish Ministry of Foreign Affairs**
w mfa.gov.tr

### EMBASSIES AND CONSULATES
**Australia**
Asker Ocağı Cad 15, Elmadağ, Şişli
( (0212) 243 13 33
**UK**
MAP J5 ■ Meşrutiyet Cad 34, Tepebaşı, Beyoğlu
( (0212) 334 64 00
**US**
İstinye Mahallesi, Kaplıcalar Mevkii No. 2, İstinye
( (0212) 335 90 00

### TRAVEL SAFETY ADVICE
**Australia**
Department of Foreign Affairs and Trade
w dfat.gov.au/
w smartraveller.gov.au/
**UK**
Foreign and Commonwealth Office
w gov.uk/foreign-travel-advice
**US**
US Department of State
w travel.state.gov/

### EMERGENCY SERVICES
**Police**
( 155
**Ambulance and General Emergencies**
( 112
**Fire**
( 110

### HEALTH SERVICES
**Alman Hastanesi**
MAP L5 ■ Sıraselviler Cad 119, Taksim
( (0212) 293 21 50

**Amerikan Hastanesi**
Güzelbahçe Sok 20, Nişantaşı
( (0212) 444 37 77
w amerikanhastanesi.org

**Cerrahpaşa Hastanesi**
Koca Mustafapaşa Cad, Cerrahpaşa
( (0212) 414 30 00
w ctf.edu.tr
MAP F3 ■ Bereketzade Medresesi Sok 7, Galata
( (0212) 292 62 22
w sjh.com.tr

**Prodent-Can Ergene**
Valikonağı Cad 109/5, Nişantaşı
( (0212) 230 46 35
w prodent.com.tr

**Reha Sezgin**
Halaskargazi Cad 48/9, Harbiye
( (0212) 240 33 22

### PERSONAL SECURITY
**Tourist Police**
MAP R4 ■ Yerebatan Cad 6, Sultanahmet
( (0212) 527 45 03
w iem.gov.tr
**UK Foreign Office**
w fco.gov.uk (UK)

## Disabled Travellers

On the whole, the city is difficult to navigate in a wheelchair. Older, historic buildings tend to be totally or partially inaccessible and many mosques refuse access to wheelchairs. But the biggest problem is Istanbul itself – with its seven, often steep, hills and cobbled roads and pavements. The **Turkish Culture and Tourism Office (UK)** in London has a helpful website for disabled travellers.

## Gay Travellers

Homosexuality is not illegal in Turkey, but it is frowned upon by Islam. There is a thriving gay scene in Istanbul, but locals are not always far out of the closet and there is significant homophobia. There are many safe venues in Beyoğlu. Some useful websites are listed in the Directory opposite.

## Tourist Information

There are several official tourist offices and kiosks around the city. The one in arrivals in Atatürk Airport is open 24 hours daily; the most convenient for the majority of visitors is in Sultanahmet, near the Hippodrome, open 9am–5pm daily. Staff speak English and have useful free city maps.

For general tourist information about the city, the **Turkish Ministry of Tourism and Culture** has useful websites, and **Turkey Travel Planner** is a good independent one. For booking tickets to shows and events, **Biletix** is indispensable.

## Currency and Banking

The Turkish lira (₺) comes in 5, 10, 20, 50, 100 and 200 lira notes and 1 lira coins. One lira is split into 100 kuruş, which come in 1, 5, 10, 25 and 50 kuruş coins. You are allowed to bring unlimited foreign currency and up to US$5,000 worth of lira into Turkey, but you'll get a better exchange rate in Turkey. Note that the ₺ sign, introduced in 2012, is widely used, but many places still use the old TL (Türk Lirası) shorthand, e.g 5 TL.

Make sure that you have plenty of small-denomination notes and coins with you at all times for when you need to make small purchases. Most souvenir shops are happy to accept lira, US dollars, euros or pounds sterling. Your change will come in lira.

There are plenty of banks in the city but changing money can be slow. The many 24-hour cash dispensers (ATMs) accept all Maestro and Cirrus bank cards with a PIN, and will also give a cash advance on credit cards. Most ATMs are programmed with several languages; some even pay out in a range of currencies.

If you have cash to exchange, the best place to go is an exchange office (döviz). These kiosks are found in all the main tourist areas. They are faster and usually offer a better rate of exchange than the banks. Most outlets dealing with tourists will accept major credit cards such as Visa and MasterCard.

## Telephone and Internet

Turkey's mobile phone system is compatible with UK phones, but US cell phones may not work. To save on charges, buy a local pay-as-you-go SIM card or an international card. The few remaining public phones accept credit cards or a phone card bought from a post office. Hotel phones are usually expensive.

The international dialling code for Turkey is +90. Istanbul has two area codes: 0212 for the European side and 0216 for the Asian side. To call abroad from Istanbul, dial 00 followed by the country code (61 for Australia, 1 for the United States and 44 for the UK).

Virtually all Istanbul's hotels have free Wi-Fi, though some upmarket international chains do charge for the service. Most have a fixed terminal as well. Many of the city's cafés now have free Wi-Fi.

## Postal Services

Post offices and boxes can be recognized by a yellow and blue PTT (Post Telegraf Telefon) logo. Stamps can only be bought at post offices and **PTT** kiosks. The most useful post offices for visitors are the **Old City Post Office** and the **Beyoğlu Post Office**, both open 8.30am–7pm daily. The post can be slow, so if you wish to send purchases home, use a courier. All the main courier firms have offices in Istanbul and there are also some reliable domestic ones.

## TV, Radio and Newspapers

TVs are standard in the majority of Istanbul hotels. Most show BBC World, CNN and other international news channels, and many also show entertainment channels such as BBC Entertainment, National Geographic and the Discovery Channel.

There are three English-language Turkish daily newspapers, the *Hürriyet Daily News*, *Today's Zaman* and *Daily Sabah*. Magazine-wise, *The Guide Istanbul* (bimonthly) and *Time Out* (monthly) have entertainment and dining listings. *Cornucopia* covers the arts, history and general culture of Turkey.

## Language and Religion

In tourist areas, there will always be someone who speaks some English. Written Turkish uses the Western alphabet, but there are some differences in pronunciation. C is pronounced "*j*" as in "jam", ç is "*ch*" as in "church" and ş is "*sh*" as in "shut". İ is used as in "igloo"; the dotless "i" (ı) is more like "*uh*". The ğ is silent, but is used to draw out the preceding vowel. Ninety-nine per cent of Turks are Muslim, but the degree to which they practise their religion varies greatly.

## Opening Hours and Public Holidays

Banks in main tourist areas open 8:30am–5pm Monday to Friday; a few larger branches also open on Saturday mornings – all have 24-hour cash dispensers. Post offices open 9am–5pm Monday to Saturday. Shops are open 10am–6pm Monday to Saturday, with many tourist shops and larger shops open longer. Malls open 10am–10pm.

Museum and sight opening times vary markedly, though 9am–5pm is a useful guideline. The majority of the more important museums and attractions such as Haghia Sophia and Topkapı Place are open by an hour or two longer between April and October than they are between November and March.

There are five official one-day state holidays; 1 January is New Year's Day, 23 April is National Sovereignty & Children's Day, 19 May is Youth & Sports Day, 30 August is Victory Day and 29 October is Republic Day.

There are two principal religious festivals: Şeker Bayramı, which follows the holy month of Ramazan (Ramadan), and Kurban Bayramı *(see p57)*. During Ramazan, no water or food is allowed during daylight hours. Nothing actually shuts down, but daily life is disrupted. The dates of Ramazan, Şeker Bayramı and Kurban Bayramı move backwards by 11 days each year.

## Electrical Appliances

The current is 220V, and plugs have two round pins. You'll need a transformer to use 110V appliances from the US.

## DIRECTORY

### DISABLED TRAVELLERS

**Turkish Culture and Tourism Office (UK)**
w gototurkey.co.uk

### GAY TRAVELLERS

w gaysofturkey.com
w hipsultan.com
w istanbulgay.com

### TOURIST INFORMATION

**Biletix**
w biletix.com

**Tourist Office**
MAP Q4 ■ Divanyolu 3, Sultanahmet
c (0212) 518 87 54

**Turkey Travel Planner**
w turkeytravelplanner.com

**Turkish Ministry of Tourism and Culture**
w gototurkey.co.uk
w kultur.gov.tr

### TELEPHONE AND INTERNET

w travelsim.co.uk

### POSTAL SERVICES

**Aras**
c 444 2552
w araskargo.com.tr

**Beyoğlu Post Office**
MAP K5 ■ Yeni Çarşı Cad, Beyoğlu
c (0212) 251 51 50

**Old City Post Office**
MAP Q2 ■ Büyük Postane Cad, Sirkeci
c (0212) 526 12 00

**PTT**
w ptt.gov.tr

**Yurtiçi**
c 444 9999
w yurticikargo.com

### NEWSPAPERS AND MAGAZINES

w hurriyetdailynews.com
w todayszaman.com
w dailysabah.com
w theguideistanbul.com
w timeoutistanbul.com

## Weather

Summers are sunny and dry, with the odd thunderstorm. It can reach 40° C (104° F), but 31–33° C (88–91° F) is normal at noon in August, dropping to around 23° C (74° F) at night. Winter can be cool and damp, with some snow and January temperatures of around 8° C (46° F) at midday and 2° C (36° F) overnight. In April, May, June and September/October, the weather is ideal for exploring on foot.

## Toilets

There are still relatively few modern public conveniences (*bay* for men, *bayan* for women) in Istanbul. Some have squat toilets only. Carry tissues, as there may not always be paper. Most mosques have squat toilets attached. There is usually a charge of around ₺1 to use these facilities. Most sights, cafés and restaurants have Western-style toilets.

## Time Difference

Turkey is 2 hours ahead of Greenwich Mean Time.

## Shopping

Traditionally, Istanbulites shop in bazaars. Most famous is the historic **Grand Bazaar,** a covered "mall" of over 4,000 shops dating back several hundred years. It's full of everything from fine quality Turkish carpets and jewellery to fake designer goods and touristy souvenirs. The Egyptian Bazaar, also known as the Spice Bazaar is equally venerable and is excellent for spices, dried fruit and nuts and much more. The Arasta Bazaar is good for authentic souvenirs such as İznik pottery and *peştemal* (*hamam* towels). Haggling in places like this is part of daily life. Take your time, shop around and don't feel pressurized. When you are ready, offer half the price and take it from there.

For European-style clothes shopping, head across the Golden Horn to İstiklal Caddesi, or to the posh suburbs of Nisantaşı and Teşvikiye. The best and/or most convenient of the city's 90 malls are **Kanyon**, the **Zorlu Centre**, **City's Mall** or **Demirören**. Don't bargain for goods in upmarket shops or shopping malls.

VAT (*KDV* in Turkish) is included in fixed-price goods. There are various rates, but the most common is 18 per cent. Prices may rise if you ask for a VAT invoice – a trader who writes an invoice will have to pay tax. To reclaim tax on departure, shop at places displaying a tax-free sign and get a Global Refund Cheque to reclaim the tax (in cash) at the airport. You may be asked to produce the goods, so keep them with you.

## Dining

The very finest of Turkey's renowned cuisine can be found in the metropolis of Istanbul. Eating places in Sultanahmet are not always the greatest – try to head further afield for a more authentic Istanbul culinary experience. Children are welcomed in all but the smartest places, but don't expect highchairs.

*Lokantas* are day-to-day eateries. They range from self-service cafeterias to full-service brasserie-style places, invariably serving stew-type dishes from steam trays, though they often have grills as well. Prices are affordable; few serve alcohol. A *restoran* is upmarket; if the word *balık* is included, the place specializes in fish and seafood. A *kebapcı* serves kebabs and *lahmacun*, a thin, round flatbread with a savoury mince topping; a *dönerci*, döner kebabs and other roast meats. A *pideci* is the Turkish equivalent of a pizzeria, though the Turkish *pide* does not have a tomato sauce layer; it is usually cheese or meat only.

For a drink and live music with a meal, usually an array of *meze* (Turkish tapas) followed by grilled fish, try a *meyhane*. To try a hookah pipe, head for a *nargile* café, where you'll be plied with sweet tea while you suck on a waterpipe. Simple *kahvehanes* (tearooms) are generally a male preserve, where men spend their time playing games of backgammon. Some cafés have a separate section for women and families (*aile salonu*) at the back, as do some restaurants.

Turks usually eat desserts separately to main meals; a *muhallebici* sells milk puddings; *pastanes* sell pastries, such as baklava. Look out for patisseries where you can sit down and sample baklava or cake with a shot of Turkish coffee.

Bars in Sultanahmet are very touristy; head across the Golden Horn to Galata and Beyoğlu for lively drinking joints ranging from studenty dives to chic rooftop bars.

Few restaurants in Istanbul cater specifically to vegetarians, though there are few places in Beyoğlu. Good options for vegetarians are *pide*, Turkish pizzas dripping with a Cheddar-cheese-type topping, or goat's cheese with parsley. The stews and soups sold at *lokantas* are often virtually vegetarian, but usually have a meat stock. There are dozens of veggie *meze* in decent *meyhanes*.

If a service charge *(servis dahil)* isn't added to your bill, leave 10 per cent.

Istanbul has become fashionable for culinary courses and food tours; see below for details.

## Trips and Tours

Most travel agents and tour operators in Turkey will be happy to provide a private guide in one of half a dozen major languages. The guide should be accredited by the Ministry of Tourism. Some licensed guides (check the ID around their necks) tout for business outside major sights.

Many agencies offer tours by bus, boat, on foot or a mix of all three, with full- and half-day options. Reliable companies for cultural tours include offer offbeat culinary tours, **Cooking Alaturka** Turkish cookery classes. **Big Bus City Tours** do

open-topped double-decker hop-on, hop-off tours of the city.

## Where to stay

On the whole, the standard of accommo-dation is high, and most places are good value. Sultanahmet and some areas adjoining it are Istanbul tourist heartland, and there are several hundred hotels here. Options range from cheap-and-cheerful hostels to luxury hotels, boutique hotels fashioned from period Ottoman town houses and not especially characterful hotels that are comfortable and well run. Across the Golden Horn in Galata and Beyoğlu are many more choices, ranging from hip hostels to late 19th-century European-style hotels such as the famed Pera Palace (see p83). There are lots of apartments for rent here too. This district is usually favoured by those as interested in shopping, dining and gallery-hopping as they are by historic sights. Period luxury hotels fronting the Bosphorus are very popular and expensive.

## Rates and Booking

It pays to book early, as many hotels now work on a yield-management system. A lot of hotels also offer decent discounts for bookings made through their own website (though this doesn't mean you can't find a better buy on one of the standard online booking sites, such as

Expedia) and for bookings paid by cash. Room prices tend to drop dramatically out of season (November to early March, excluding Christmas and New Year).

## DIRECTORY

### SHOPPING

**City's Mall**
Teşvikiye Cad 162, Nişantaşı
🅦 citysnisantasi.com

**Demirören**
MAP K4 ▪ İstiklal Cad, Beyoğlu
🅦 demirorenistiklal.com

**Grand Bazaar**
🅦 grandbazaaristanbul.org

**Kanyon**
Büyükdere Cad 185, Levent
🅦 kanyon.com.tr

**Zorlu Centre**
Zincirlikuyu
🅦 zorlucenter.com

### TRIPS AND TOURS

**Big Bus City Tours**
MAP R4 ▪ Ayasofya Karşısı 1, Sultanahmet
📞 (0212) 283 13 96
🅦 bigbustours.com

**Cooking Alaturka**
MAP R5 ▪ Akbıyık Cad 72/A, Sultanahmet
🅦 cookingalaturka.com

**Fest Travel**
Barbaros Bulvarı 74, Balmucu
📞 (0212) 216 10 36
🅦 festtravel.com.tr

**Istanbul Walks**
MAP Q5 ▪ Şifahamamı Sok, Sultanahmet
📞 (0212) 516 63 00
🅦 istanbulwalks.net

**Istanbul Tour Studio**
MAP G2 ▪ Necatibey Cad 97, Beyoğlu
📞 (0533) 355 30 49
🅦 istanbultourstudio.com

**Istanbul Eats**
🅦 istanbuleats.com.tr

# Places to Stay

**PRICE CATEGORIES**
For a standard, double room per night (with breakfast if included), taxes and extra charges.
.....................................................

₺ under ₺200   ₺₺ ₺200–400   ₺₺₺ over ₺400

## Luxury Hotels

### Ceylan InterContinental, Taksim
MAP B5 ■ Asker Ocağı Cad 1 ■ (0212) 368 44 44 ■ www.istanbul.inter continental.com.tr ■ ₺₺₺
This hilltop tower offers some of the finest views in the city. It has 382 rooms and suites, plus a bar, restaurants, health club and 24-hour business centre. Join Istanbul high society for tea with live music in the botanic garden or tea lounge.

### Conrad Istanbul, Beşiktaş
MAP C5 ■ Saray Cad 5 ■ (0212) 310 25 25 ■ www. conradistanbul.com ■ ₺₺₺
Each of the 590 rooms in this huge hotel has a view. The facilities are second to none, and the furnishings chic. Its bars and restaurants offer Italian and Turkish cuisine.

### Eresin Crown, Sultanahmet
MAP Q6 ■ Küçük Ayasofya Cad 40 ■ (0212) 638 44 28 ■ www.eresin crown.com.tr ■ ₺₺₺
Standing on the site of the great Byzantine Palace, this truly luxurious hotel even has its own museum. All 60 rooms and suites have parquet floors

and Jacuzzi baths. There are two restaurants, a bar and a terrace that offers lovely sea views.

### Four Seasons Hotel, Sultanahmet
MAP R5 ■ Tevkifhane Sok 1 ■ (0212) 402 30 00 ■ www.fourseasons.com ■ ₺₺₺
The sheer opulence of the Four Seasons belies its past as an Ottoman prison. The 65 rooms are furnished with antiques and kilims, there is a health club, a magnificent glass-roofed restaurant and superb views over the Sea of Marmara.

### Hyatt Regency, Taksim
MAP B5 ■ Taşkışla Cad ■ (0212) 368 12 34 ■ www.hyatt.com ■ ₺₺₺
A resort hotel with 360 rooms and suites, plus health club, pool, tennis courts and business facilities. Elegant decor and great views.

### Marmara Pera Tepebaşı
MAP J5 ■ Meşrutiyet Cad ■ (0212) 334 03 00 ■ www.themarmara hotels. com ■ ₺₺₺
In the heart of Beyoğlu, with a signature café-restaurant and rooftop pool, this chic hotel has fabulous floor-to-ceiling windows in every room.

### Park Hyatt, Teşvikiye
MAP B4 ■ Bronz Sok 4, Teşvikiye ■ (0212) 315 12 34 ■ www.istanbul. park.hyatt.com ■ ₺₺₺
Located in a busy shopping district, this stylish boutique hotel has 90 spacious rooms and suites. There is also a spa and a fitness centre.

### Raffles Istanbul
MAP C4 ■ Zorlu Centre, Zincirlikuyu ■ (0212) 924 02 00 ■ www.raffles.com/ Istanbul ■ ₺₺₺
Part of a contemporary shopping and performing arts centre, Raffles is luxury incarnate. Many rooms have a Bosphorus panorama. Personal butlers attend to guests' needs and there is a Michelin-star Spanish restaurant attached.

### Ritz-Carlton, Şişli
MAP B5 ■ Süzer Plaza, Elmadağ ■ (0212) 334 44 44 ■ www.ritzcarlton.com ■ ₺₺₺
"Ritz" is a byword for luxury, and the Istanbul hotel's 244 rooms and suites more than live up to expectation. There's a whisky and cigar bar too.

## Large Upmarket Hotels

### Ataköy Marina Hotel
Sahilyolu ■ (0212) 560 41 10 ■ www.atakoymarina-hotel.com.tr ■ ₺₺₺
Situated on the shores of the Sea of Marmara in the Bakırköy district, the Ataköy Marina Hotel is only 8 km (5 miles) from Ataturk Airport. Facilities include tennis courts, swimming pool and meeting rooms. There is a shuttle bus to Sultanahmet.

### Best Western Eresin Taxim Hotel, Taksim

MAP B5 ■ Topçu Cad 16 ■ (0212) 256 08 03 ■ www. eresintaxim.com.tr ■ ₺₺₺
You can even get hypoallergenic pillows at this four-star hotel. The 70 rooms and suites include some triples. The lounge bar has live piano music in the evenings.

### Germir Palas

MAP Y2 ■ Cumhuriyet Cad 7, Taksim ■ (0212) 361 11 10 ■ www. germirpalas.com ■ ₺₺₺
The entrance to this town-centre gem on Beyoğlu's main street is easy to miss. The lobby and bars are plush, and the rooms are well decorated with interesting textiles. The terrace restaurant is great in summer and boasts fine views over the Bosphorus.

### Hilton Hotel, Harbiye

MAP B5 ■ Cumhuriyet Cad ■ (0212) 315 60 00 ■ www.hilton.com ■ ₺₺₺
Conveniently located for Taksim and the business districts, this grand hotel has 498 rooms, fitness centre, tennis courts, two pools, *hamam*, conference facilities and much more.

### The Marmara Istanbul, Taksim

MAP L4 ■ Taksim Meydanı ■ (0212) 334 83 00 ■ www.taksim.the marmarahotels.com ■ ₺₺₺
This large, modern hotel situated on Taksim Square offers 376 comfortable rooms with city views, as well as a fully equipped gym, outdoor pool, *hamam* and several top-class restaurants.

### Mövenpick Hotel Istanbul, Levent

MAP U2 ■ Büyükdere Cad 4, Levent ■ (0212) 319 29 29 ■ www.moven pickhotels.com ■ ₺₺₺
This hilltop hotel with 249 rooms and suites offers great views and slick service. The lobby café serves sumptuous chocolates, cakes and Mövenpick ice cream.

### Radisson Blu Bosphorus Hotel, Ortaköy

MAP C4 ■ Çırağan Cad 46 ■ (0212) 310 15 00 ■ www. radissonsas.com ■ ₺₺₺
The location is the real winner – the peaceful village of Ortaköy, beside the Bosphorus.This hotel has a patio restaurant overlooking the water, and 120 rooms with contemporary decor. Allow plenty of time for taxis into town during rush hour.

### Renaissance Polat Istanbul Hotel, Yeşilyurt

Sahilyolu Cad 2 ■ (0212) 414 18 00 ■ www.polat renaissance.com ■ ₺₺₺
Located close to the airport and World Trade Centre, this 416-room hotel has a luxury pool and health club. There are also fine restaurants, bars and cafés, and good business facilities.

### Swissôtel The Bosphorus, Maçka

MAP B5 ■ Bayıldım Cad 2 ■ (0212) 326 11 00 ■ www.istanbul.swissotel. com ■ ₺₺₺
On a hilltop with views of the Bosphorus, this hotel has 585 rooms and suites, a wellness centre, shopping arcade, restaurants and rooftop bars.

### Taxim Suites, Taksim

MAP B5 ■ Cumhuriyet Cad 31 ■ (0212) 254 77 77 ■ www.taximsuites.com ■ ₺₺₺
These 20 fully serviced suites are good high-end value for those who need a bit more space, giving you a one-bed apartment for less than the cost of a five-star hotel room. With Taksim Square on the doorstep, there are plenty of places to eat nearby.

## Characterful Hotels – Sultanahmet and the Old City

### Best Western Acropol Hotel

MAP R5 ■ Akbıyık Cad 21 ■ (0212) 638 90 21 ■ www.book.best western.com ■ ₺₺
The 28 rooms in this restored Ottoman house have wooden floors and painted ceilings – but also Wi-Fi and double glazing. The fifth-floor restaurant has fine views. Free airport transfers for guests.

### Blue House Hotel

MAP R5 ■ Dalbastı Sok 14 ■ (0212) 638 90 10 ■ www. bluehouse.com.tr ■ ₺₺
In a quiet street behind the Arasta Bazaar, this hotel has 26 rooms, all with superb views.

### Hotel Dersaadet

MAP Q6 ■ Küçük Ayasofya Cad, Kapıağası Sok 5 ■ (0212) 458 07 60/1 ■ www.hoteldersaadet. com ■ ₺₺
Its name means "place of felicity and beauty" – perfect for this Ottoman house at the foot of the hill behind Sultanahmet Square. There are superb views of the old city or the sea from all 17 rooms.

### Hotel Empress Zöe
MAP R5 ▪ Akbıyık Cad 10, Sultanahmet ▪ (0212) 518 43 60/25 04 ▪ www. emzoe.com ▪ ₺₺
Old houses surround a lush garden and ruins of a 15th-century bathhouse at this delightful hotel. Its 25 rooms and suites are decorated in Turkish style.

### Hotel Kariye, Edirnekapı
MAP J2 ▪ Kariye Camii Sok 6 ▪ (0212) 534 84 14 ▪ www.kariyeotel.com ▪ ₺₺
This late 19th-century wooden mansion has 27 rooms and suites (with modern amenities), a garden overlooking the Golden Horn and renowned restaurant Asitane (see p79).

### Hotel Kybele
MAP R4 ▪ Yerebatan Cad 35 ▪ (0212) 511 77 66/7 ▪ www.kybelehotel.com ▪ ₺₺
Intimate, family-run and friendly, and a couple of steps from Divanyolu, this Aladdin's cave of a hotel is a treasure trove of Turkish history, with hundreds of lamps and other Ottoman antiques decorating the public rooms, 16 bedrooms and garden.

### Hotel Sarı Konak
MAP R5 ▪ Mimar Mehmet Ağa Cad 26 ▪ (0212) 638 62 58 ▪ www.istanbul hotelsairkonak.com ▪ ₺₺
The owners of this 19-room hotel pride themselves on providing a "home from home". The café has 360° views, and breakfast is served in a Byzantine courtyard.

### Ibrahim Pasha
MAP Q5 ▪ Terzihane Sok, 5 Adliye Yanı ▪ (0212) 518 03 94 ▪ www.ibrahimpasha.com ▪ ₺₺
A couple of 19th-century town houses, on a side street running off the historic Hippodrome, have been converted into a superb, ultra-friendly boutique hotel. Room decor combines Ottoman opulence with contemporary elegance. Downstairs is a lounge area, an open fire and a library.

### Sarnıç Hotel
MAP Q6 ▪ Küçük Ayasofya Cad 26 ▪ (0212) 518 23 23 ▪ www.sarnichotel.com ▪ ₺₺
This 21-room hotel behind the Blue Mosque has a lovely rooftop terrace restaurant. Guests can see the magnificent 5th-century Byzantine cistern (sarnıç) under the hotel.

### Ayasofya Konakları
MAP R4 ▪ Soğukçeşme Sok ▪ (0212) 513 36 60 ▪ www.ayasofya konaklari.com ▪ ₺₺₺
The first of the "special hotels" in Sultanahmet, this stretches along nine restored houses and has 64 rooms. There's a café and a restaurant on site.

## Characterful Hotels – Galata, Beyoğlu and around

### Eklektik Guesthouse, Galata
MAP F2 ▪ Kadribey Cikmazı 4, Serdari Ekrem Cad ▪ (0212) 243 74 46 ▪ www.eklektikgalata.com ▪ ₺
A funky guesthouse in a restored Ottoman house, this has seven rooms

decorated in styles from 1960s retro to colonial.

### Hotel Villa Zurich, Cihangir
MAP G2 ▪ Akarsu Yokuşu Cad 36 ▪ (0212) 293 06 04 ▪ www.hotelvillazurich.com ▪ ₺
A short walk from Taksim Square, this 42-room hotel has a breakfast terrace with Bosphorus views.

### Anemon Galata, Beyoğlu
MAP F2 ▪ Büyük Hendek Cad 5, Kuledibi ▪ (0212) 293 23 43 ▪ www.anemonhotels.com ▪ ₺₺
This 27-room hotel in a restored Art Nouveau mansion is just a short walk from Beyoğlu's shopping and nightlife.

### Galatasaray House Hotel
MAP K5 ▪ Bostanbaşı Cad 19, Çukurcuma ▪ (0212) 244 34 00 ▪ www.househotel.com ▪ ₺₺
This 1870s building is located in the quiet side streets beneath İstiklal Caddesi. The block has been converted into a stylish hotel with high-ceilinged rooms, wooden floors and chrome showers. Great views from the top-floor.

### Mama Shelter
MAP K4 ▪ İstiklal Cad 50-54, Beyoğlu ▪ (0212) 252 01 00 ▪ www.mamashelter.com ▪ ₺₺
Occupying the top floor of İstiklal Caddesi's swish Demirören mall (see p110), this French-Turkish concept hotel brings a bit of good-value sophistication and fun to the city's hotel scene. All-white rooms are offset by cartoon masks over light fittings

and exposed brick walls. There's a restaurant-bar-club attached.

## Niles Hotel
MAP E5 ■ Dibekli Cami Sok 13 ■ (0212) 517 32 39 ■ www.hotelniles.com ■ ₺₺
Located near the main tourist areas of Sultanahmet, this hotel offers great value with compact yet tasteful rooms, an excellent roof-top restaurant with sea views and friendly staff.

## SuB
Necatibey Cad 21, Karaköy ■ (0212) 243 00 05 ■ www.subkarakoy.com ■ ₺₺
The rooms are individually designed with a mix of industrial grunge and homely touches, such as wraparound headboards and natural pine floors. Excellent terrace bar and café complete the picture.

## Triada Residence
MAP L4 ■ Meşelik Sok 4, İstiklal Cad ■ (0212) 251 01 01 ■ www.triada.com.tr ■ ₺₺
Great location opposite the monumental Greek Orthodox Church of Haghia Triada. The cosy but contemporary rooms have pale walls adorned with tasteful prints and photographs, contrasting with heavily grained wooden floors and furniture. Large flat-screen TVs in all rooms.

## 10 Karaköy
Kemeraltı Cad 10, Karaköy ■ (0212) 703 33 33 ■ www.morganshotelgroup.com ■ ₺₺₺
Located close to the Galata Bridge, the Morgan Group's first venture in Istanbul is fashioned from a 19th-century

Neo-Classical building that combines sleek decor with period style. Elegant roof bar.

## Tom Tom Suites
MAP K6 ■ Tomtom Kaptan Sk 18 ■ (0212) 292 49 49 ■ www.tomtomsuites.com ■ ₺₺₺
Occupying a former Franciscan nunnery, Tom Tom Suites provide some of the most stylish rooms in Beyoğlu. Located opposite the Italian consulate on a quiet street, the rooms have en-suite bathrooms with marble-clad walls, high-ceilings and muted contemporary furnishings. Some upper-floor rooms have lovely Bosphorus views.

## Vault Karaköy
MAP F3 ■ Bankalar Cad 5, Karaköy ■ (0212) 244 34 00 ■ www.thehousehotel.com ■ ₺₺₺
A grandiose 19th-century bank in hip Karaköy has been converted into a boutique hotel run by the well-regarded House group. Many original features have been retained, including granite floors and tall, elegant windows. The vault itself is now stocked with fine wines.

## Budget Hotels and Self-Catering

## Agora Guest House and Hostel
MAP R5 ■ Amiral Tafdil Sok 6 ■ (0212) 458 55 47 ■ www.agoraguesthouse.com ■ ₺
The Agora blurs the lines between small budget hotel and hostel. There's a comfy communal living room/breakfast area, with computers, a huge TV and

great terrace. Choose from mixed-sex dorms or private doubles.

## Bada Bing
Serçe Sokak 6, Karaköy ■ (0212) 249 41 11 ■ www.badabinghostel.com ■ ₺
Located in the district of Karaköy, this trendy yet well priced hostel provides air-conditioned rooms as well as four-, six- and ten-bed dormitories. The rooftop terrace offers good views.

## Büyük (Grand) Londra, Beyoğlu
MAP J5 ■ Meşrutiyet Cad 53 ■ (0212) 245 06 70 ■ www.londrahotel.net ■ ₺
Faded decadence at its most alluring, the Londra has been around since the 1900s. Ernest Hemingway stayed here and the Turkish hit film *Head On* featured the hotel. Some of the eccentrically decorated rooms overlook the Golden Horn.

## Hotel Sultanahmet, Sultanahmet
MAP Q4 ■ Divanyolu Cad 20 ■ (0212) 527 02 39 ■ www.hotelsultanahmet.com ■ ₺
A popular budget choice on the main drag, the Sultanahmet does the basics well, with clean rooms and friendly staff.

## Naz Wooden House Inn, Sultanahmet
MAP R6 ■ Akbıyık Değirmeni Sok 7 ■ (0212) 516 71 30 ■ www.nazwoodenhouseinn.com ■ ₺
This wooden bed and breakfast is right in the heart of the Old City. The seven imaginatively decorated rooms are very good value, while the roof terrace has great views.

*For a key to hotel price categories see p112*

### Peninsula

MAP G6 ▪ Adliye Sok 6, Sultanahmet ▪ (0212) 458 68 50 ▪ www.hotel-peninsula.com ▪ ₺

Well located, this boutique hotel offers great value for money. There is a lovely roof terrace that also doubles up as the breakfast room. Service is excellent.

### Rapunzel Hostel

MAP F3 ▪ Bereketzade Camii Sok 3, Galata ▪ (0212) 292 50 34 ▪ www.rapunzelistanbul.com ▪ ₺

Born out of a need to provide (mainly) younger visitors with a base in the trendy Galata district, Rapunzel offers more than the average Istanbul hostel, with en-suite dorms, hair-dryers and individual reading lights.

### Şebnem Hotel, Sultanahmet

MAP S5 ▪ Akbıyık Cad Adliye Sokak Çıkmazı 1 ▪ (0212) 517 66 23 ▪ www.sebnemhotel.net ▪ ₺

The Şebnem is a small, welcoming guest house, with 15 simply decorated rooms (including one triple and one family room).

### Side Hotel & Pension, Sultanahmet

MAP R5 ▪ Utangaç Sok 20 ▪ (0212) 517 22 82 ▪ www.sidehotel.com ▪ ₺

You can choose between a hotel room (half with air conditioning, half with fans), two self-catering apartments and a more basic pension (without air conditioning) – all side by side, and under the same

management. Close to Haghia Sophia (see pp16–17), with superb views from the roof.

### Hotel Bulvar Palace, Aksaray

MAP D5 ▪ Atatürk Bulvarı 36 ▪ (0212) 528 58 81 ▪ www.hotelbulvarpalas.com ▪ ₺₺

This is a great deal – a four-star hotel at a bargain price. The location near the Grand Bazaar is good, and the 70 rooms and 10 suites are well-equipped.

### Manzara Istanbul, Galata

MAP F2 ▪ Tatarbeyi Sok 26B ▪ (0212) 252 46 60 ▪ www.manzara-istanbul.com ▪ ₺₺

Located in the heart of the city, Manzara offers a wide range of spacious apartment options. Many have a balcony and terrace with breathtaking views over the Bosphorus.

### Pasha Place

MAP J6 ▪ Serdar-I Ekrem Cad, Galata ▪ 07729 251 676 ▪ www.istanbulplace.com ▪ ₺₺₺

Pasha Place is the most prestigious property in the roster of Anglo-Turkish partnership Istanbul!place. Like most of their other pads, it's a beautifully renovated 19th century third-floor apartment located near the Galata Tower. This one offers two spacious double bedrooms, one twin bedroom and a living room with views over the Golden Horn to the Old City, as well as a spacious kitchen, dining space and bar.

## Bosphorus and Seafront Hotels

### Anzac Hotel, Çanakkale

Saat Kulesi Meydanı 8 ▪ (0286) 217 77 77 ▪ www.anzachotel.com ▪ ₺

Travellers rave about the superb service at this small hotel, well placed for Troy and Gallipoli. There are 25 rooms, a restaurant and rooftop bar (in summer).

### Aya Nikola Butik Pansiyon, Büyükada (Princes' Islands)

MAP V6 ▪ Aya Nikola Mevki 104, Büyükada ▪ (0126) 382 41 43 ▪ www.ayanikolabutikpansiyon.com ▪ ₺₺

Right on the waterfront on charming Büyükada (see p99), the largest of the Princes' Islands, this atmospheric 11-room boutique hotel provides the perfect antidote to teeming Istanbul. Go to sleep to the sound of the water lapping against the shore a few feet away.

### Merit Halki Palace, Heybeliada (Princes' Islands)

MAP V6 ▪ Refah Şehitleri Cad 94 ▪ (0216) 351 00 25 ▪ www.halkipalacehotel.com ▪ ₺₺

A beautifully restored old wooden house, the hotel offers lovely views across Heybeliada and the Sea of Marmara from the terrace restaurant, pool and balcony. Ample opportunities for activities such as hiking, horse riding, cycling and short walks.

### Splendid Palace Hotel, Büyükada (Princes' Islands)

MAP V6 ■ 23 Nisan Cad 39 ■ (0216) 382 69 50 ■ www.splendidhotel.net ■ ₺₺

There are touches of Art Nouveau elegance in this very grand belle époque hotel, built in 1908 around a central courtyard. The 70 rooms and four suites all have balconies and wonderful views.

### A'jia

MAP U2 ■ Çubuklu Cad 27, Kanlıca ■ (0212) 413 93 00 ■ www.ajiahotel. com ■ ₺₺₺

This is a lovely conversion of a traditional wooden waterfront yalı (mansion). A'jia is a little out of the city for some, but its soothing mix of contemporary decor, informal ambience and luscious breakfast spreads in a peaceful location make it a winner.

### Bosphorus Palace, Beylerbeyi (Asian side)

MAP U3 ■ Yalıboyu Cad 64 ■ (0216) 422 00 03 ■ www.bosphoruspalace. com ■ ₺₺₺

On the banks of the Bosphorus, the restored yalı (mansion) of a 19th-century Grand Vizier. With only 14 rooms, it is intimate and glamorous – perfect for a romantic dinner. A private boat commutes to the centre.

### Çırağan Palace Kempinski, Beşiktaş

MAP C4 ■ Çırağan Cad 32 ■ (0212) 326 46 46 ■ www.kempinski.com/ istanbul ■ ₺₺₺

Its terrace lapped by the Bosphorus, this Ottoman palace has a spa, health club and two of the city's best restaurants. Most of the 313 rooms are in the modern extensions, but for a real treat take one of the 11 suites in the original palace.

### Four Seasons Bosphorus

Çırağan Cad 28, Beşiktaş ■ (0212) 381 40 00 ■ www.fourseasons.com/ bosphorus ■ ₺₺₺

If you don't fancy the Four Seasons Sultanahmet in the touristy Old City, head for this one. The setting, in a restored 19th-century palace overlooking the famous strait is an ideal choice. There are also good spas, excellent restaurants and great views.

### Grand Tarabya

MAP U2 ■ Haydar Aliyev Cad, Tarabya ■ (0212) 363 33 00 ■ www. grandttarabya.com ■ ₺₺₺

Out in the smart Bosphorus-front suburb of Tarabya (ancient Therapia) this hotel, right on a little bay of the famous strait, offers contemporary-styled rooms, good dining and a stunning spa with floor-to-ceiling glass windows that command stunning views over the Bosphorus.

### House Hotel Bosphorus

Salahane Sok 1, Ortaköy ■ (0212) 327 77 87 ■ www.thehousehotel. com ■ ₺₺₺

Restored by the design team Autobahn, this hotel occupies a lovely 19th-century mansion on the waterfront. Some rooms even have superb views of the strait to Asia.

### Les Ottomans

MAP C4 ■ Muallim Naci Cad 68 ■ (0212) 359 15 00 ■ www.lesottomans.com ■ ₺₺₺

One of the city's most exclusive (and most expensive) hotels. Housed in an old waterfront mansion, it is noted for its architecture. Guests can admire superlative Bosphorus views, head down the strait on a hotel boat, relax in the Caudalie spa or fine-dine at Şamadan restaurant.

### Shangri-La Bosphorus

MAP C5 ■ Hayrettin İskelesi Sk, Beşiktaş ■ (0212) 275 88 88 ■ www. shangri-la.com/Istanbul ■ ₺₺₺

Fashioned from an old tobacco factory this prestigious Bosphorus front hotel is made up of 186 rooms. Rooms are plush and suites have stunning views across to the Old City. As you might expect, Far Eastern (Cantonese) cuisine is a big feature here. The only downside is the lack of extensive grounds.

### Sumahan on the Water, Çengelköy (Asian side)

MAP U3 ■ Kuleli Cad 43 ■ (0216) 422 80 00 ■ www. sumahan.com ■ ₺₺₺

Magnificently converted from an old rakı distillery by its architect owners, the 18-room Sumahan on the Asian shore of the Bosphorus is fast getting a reputation as one of Istanbul's best small hotels. Perhaps not the best sightseeing base (although the hotel runs shuttle boats), it is ideal for a romantic break.

*For a key to hotel price categories* see p112

# Istanbul

# Acknowledgments

## Author

Melissa Shales is an award-winning travel writer. As author, contributor or editor she has worked on more than 100 guide-books. She has written travel articles for many magazines, and was editor of *Traveller* magazine. During 2004-06 she was Chairman of the British Guild of Travel Writers.

The author would like to thank the following for their generosity, hard work and patience during the research of this book: the Turkish Tourist Office, particularly Joanna Marsh in London and Ilginay Altuntaş in Istanbul; Emma Levine; and Victoria Gooch.

**Additional contributor**
Terry Richardson

**Publishing Director** Georgina Dee

**Publisher** Vivien Antwi

**Design Director** Phil Ormerod

**Editorial** Michelle Crane, Rachel Fox, Freddie Marriage, Fíodhna Ní Ghríofa, Scarlett O'Hara, Marianne Petrou, Sally Schafer,

**Revisions** Emma Brady, Bharti Karakoti, Terry Richardson, Aakanksha Singh

**Design** Richard Czapnik, Sunita Gahir, Bharti Karakoti

**Picture Research** Phoebe Lowndes, Susie Peachey, Ellen Root, Oran Tarjan

**Cartography** Jasneet Arora, Suresh Kumar, Casper Morris, Simonetta Giori, Dominic Beddow

**DTP** Jason Little, George Nimmo

**Production** Linda Dare

**Factchecker** Terry Richardson

**Proofreader** Nikky Twyman

**Indexer** Helen Peters

**Illustrator** Chapel Design & Marketing

First edition created by Coppermill Books, London

**Commissioned Photography** Christopher and Sally Gable, Rough Guides/Lydia Evans, Rough Guides/ Roger Mapp, Tony Souter, Clive Streeter, Francesca Yorke.

## Picture Credits

The publisher would like to thank the following for their kind permission to reproduce their photographs:
**Key:** a-above; b-below/bottom; c-centre; f-far; l-left; r-right; t-top

**360istanbul:** 53tr.

**4Corners:** Sime/Anna Serrano 3tl, 24-5, 58-9; Sime/Stefano Scatà 30-1.

**Akdeniz Hatay Sofrasi:** Tenten's Vaio 52cr.

**Alamy Images:** AgencyWestend61 GmbH/ Martin Siepmann 55bl; blickwinkel 74tl; David Coleman 21bl, 90tl; Ian G Dagnall 14cla; Oguz Dikbakan 97tl; Mark Eveleigh 100bl; Tim Graham 73tr; Hackenberg-Photo-Cologne 27clb; Chris Hellier 92br; Heritage Image Partnership Ltd/Fine Art Images *The capture of Constantinople by land and sea in 1204. Miniature from the Historia by William of Tyre, 1460s by Anonymous* 38bl; imageBROKER/ Martin Siepmann 98crb; JL Photography 33cr; Michael Kemp 20bl; ZUMA Press, Inc. 78br.

**Ali Muhiddin Haci Bekir:** 87br.

**Asitane:** 52tl, 79tr.

**Bridgeman Images:** National Gallery, London/ *The Sultan Mehmet II (1480) by Gentile Bellini* 39tr.

**Çemberlitaş Hamamı:** 30c.

**Ciragan Palace Kempinski Istanbul, Laledan Restaurant:** 95tr.

**Corbis:** Guido Cozzi 66cr; Monique Jaques 57b; Lebrecht Music & Arts 97cb; Hans Lippert 91br; Martin Siepmann 56t; Jane Sweeney 2tl, 8-9.

**Dreamstime.com:** 11geiserm 22clb; Alessandro0770 11tr; Steve Allen 10cl, 47clb; Alyssand 11b; Anandoart 18bl; Ahmet Ihsan Ariturk 12-3, 29cr; Frank Bach 35bl; Beriliu 32cl; Murat Besler 62tl, 64tc; Artur Bogacki 20-1; Mikael Damkier 18-9; Ddkg 11cb; Dinosmichall 40crb; Sergey Dzyuba 2tr, 36-7; Elenatur 14br; Evren Kalinbacak 77cla; Rodríguez Fontoba 72c; Gavran333 51cla; Gelia 3tr, 102-3; Nadiia Gerbish 47tr; Ihsan Gercelman 17cr, 17bl, 28cl, 42bc, 49ca, 70c; Gozleme 51tr; Özgür Güvenç 43bl, 82b, 99tl; Patricia Hofmeester 12br; Jasmina 28bl, 28-9, 35cr, 92tl, 94bl; Jim Kelcher 19bl; Khorunzha 50b; Tetyana Kochneva 27br; Aleksandra Lande 7cra; Madrugaladverde 22-3; Pavle Marjanovic 29bl; Luciano Mortula 12bl; Mtr 4cla; Luba V Nel 22cl; Olha 26br; Pepe14 23tr; Petitfrere 33bc; Marek Poplawski 71clb; Saaaaa 77bl; Sakio3p 34-5, 84bc; Sailorr 60tl, 80-1; Scaliger 10crb, 18crb, 42tl, 75tr, 75b, 76t; Sergiy87 72tr; Siwsshippo 17tl; Softdreams 12cl; Nikolai Sorokin 32bl; Mikhail Starodubov 13cr; Svx94 34crb; Tolga Tezcan 69tl, 98tl; Tinamou 10cla; Alexander Tolstykh 40bl; Tomas1111 70t; Vincentsthomas 93tl; Shuo Wang 16clb; Wedmoscow 51clb; Zastavkin 61br; Minyun Zhou 7cr; Oleg Znamenskiy 4crb.

**Sultanahmet:** 67tr; Paul Thuysbaert 52bc.

**Galata House:** Bastiani 89cla.

**Getty Images:** Ayhan Altun 49b; Anadolu Agency 57tr; Ullstein Bild 39tl; DeAgostini / *Sovereign Theodora and Antonina, Belisarius' wife, detail from Theodora with her entourage, mosaic, south wall of the apse, Basilica of San Vitale, Ravenna, Emilia-Romagna. Italy (6th century)* 41tr; Fuse 27tl; Heritage Images 29tl, /Fine Art Images/Pera Museum *Women Drinking Coffee* (1720s) by Jean-Baptiste Vanmour 15b, /Hulton Fine Art Collection/ Pera Museum 15c; Angelika Hörschläger 26–7; Image Source 38tc; Izzet Keribar 54crb; Keystone 39cl; Yoray Liberman 55cla; Winfield Parks 19crb; Tetra Images 16–7; Jose Verhelst 43tr.

**Giritli Restoran:** 67clb.

**Homer Books:** 87tr.

**IKSV:** 56clb.

**Indigo Istanbul:** 88bl.

**Istanbul Archaeological Museum:** 21cra.

**Istanbul Modern:** Muhsin Akgun 44tl; Murat Germen 91t.

**Meze by Lemon Tree:** 89br.

**Nardis Jazz Club:** Tasdemir Asan 88tl.

**Pera Museum:** 44cb; *Kaplumbağa Terbiyecisi (The Tortoise Trainer)* (1906) by Osman Hamdi Bey 85cla.

**Robert Harding Picture Library:** Tibor Bognar 54tl; John Henry Claude 4cr; Eurasia 26bl; Stephen Rafferty 22br; Jose Fuste Raga 4b; Karl F. Schofmann 4clb, 32-3c, 33tl; Paul Seheult 4t; Tetra Images 1, 6cla; Michael Zegers 4cl.

**Sadberk Hanim Museum:** 45clb, 93bc.

**Salon İKSV:** aliguler 53br.

**Salt:** 45tr, 46tr.

**Cover**
Front and spine - Robert Harding Picture Library: Markus Lange.

Back - Dreamstime.com: Lanselot.

**Pull Out Map Cover**
Robert Harding Picture Library: Markus Lange.

All other images © Dorling Kindersley
For further information see:
www.dkimages.com

*As a guide to abbreviations in visitor information blocks:* **Adm** *= admission charge;* **DA** *= disabled access;* **D** *= dinner;* **L** *= lunch.*

Penguin
Random
House

Printed and bound in China

First published in Great Britain in 2007 by
Dorling Kindersley Limited
80 Strand, London WC2R 0RL

Copyright 2007, 2016 © Dorling
Kindersley Limited

A Penguin Random House Company

16 17 18 19 10 9 8 7 6 5 4 3 2 1

**Reprinted with revisions 2009, 2011, 2013, 2015, 2016**

A CIP catalogue record is available from the British Library.

ISBN 978 0 2412 0344 6

MIX
Paper from
responsible sources
FSC™ C018179

**SPECIAL EDITIONS OF
DK TRAVEL GUIDES**

DK Travel Guides can be purchased in bulk quantities at discounted prices for use in promotions or as premiums. We are also able to offer special editions and personalized jackets, corporate imprints, and excerpts from all of our books, tailored specifically to meet your own needs.

To find out more, please contact:

in the US
specialsales@dk.com

in the UK
travelguides@uk.dk.com

in Canada
specialmarkets@dk.com

in Australia
penguincorporatesales@
penguinrandomhouse.com.au

# Phrase Book

## Pronunciation

Turkish uses a Roman alphabet of 29 letters: 8 vowels and 21 consonants. Letters that differ from the English alphabet are: c, pronounced "j" as in "jolly"; ç, pronounced "ch" as in "church"; ğ, which lengthens the preceding vowel and is not pronounced; ı, pronounced "uh"; ö, pronounced "ur" (as in "further"); ş, pronounced "sh" as in "ship"; and ü, pronounced "ew" as in "few".

## In an Emergency

| | | |
|---|---|---|
| Help! | İmdat! | eem-**dat** |
| Call a doctor! | Bir doktor çağrın! | beer dok-**tor** **chah**-ruhn |
| Call an ambulance! | Bir ambulans çağrın! | beer am-boo-**lans** chah-ruhn |
| Call the police! | Polis çağrın! | po-**lees** **chah**-ruhn |
| Fire! | Yangın! | yan-**guhn** |
| Where is the nearest telephone/ hospital? | En yakın telefon/ hastane nerede? | en ya-**kuhn** teh-leh-**fon**/ has-ta-**neh** **neh**-reh-deh |

## Communication Essentials

| | | |
|---|---|---|
| Yes | Evet | eh-**vet** |
| No | Hayır | h-**'eye'**-uhr |
| Thank you | Teşekkür ederim | teh-shek-**kewr** **eh**-deh-reem |
| Please | Lütfen | **lewt**-fen |
| Excuse me | Affedersiniz | af-feh-der-see-neez |
| Hello | Merhaba | **mer**-ha-ba |
| Goodbye | Hoşça kalın | hosh-**cha** **ka**-luhn |
| Morning | Sabah | sa-**bah** |
| Afternoon | Öğleden sonra | ur-leh-**den** **son**-ra |
| Evening | Akşam | ak-**sham** |
| Yesterday | Dün | dewn |
| Today | Bugün | **boo**-gewn |
| Tomorrow | Yarın | **ya**-ruhn |
| Here | Burada | **boo**-ra-da |
| There | Şurada | **shoo**-ra-da |
| What? | Ne? | neh |
| When? | Ne zaman? | neh **za**-man |
| Where? | Nerede? | **neh**-reh-deh |

## Useful Phrases

| | | |
|---|---|---|
| Pleased to meet you | Memnun oldum | mem-**noon** ol-doom |
| Where is/are? | Nerede? | **neh**-reh-deh |
| How far is it to? | Ne kadar uzaktı? | neh **ka**-dar oo-zak-ta |
| Do you speak English? | İngilizce biliyor musunuz? | een-gee-**leez**-jeh bee-**lee**-yor moo-soo-nooz |
| I don't understand | Anlamıyorum | an-**la**-muh-yo-room |
| Can you help me? | Bana yardım edebilir misiniz? | ba-na yar-**duhm** eh-deh-bee-**leer** mee-see-neez |
| I don't want | istemiyorum | ees-**teh**-mee-yo room |

## Useful Words

| | | |
|---|---|---|
| big | büyük | bew-**yewk** |
| small | küçük | kew-**chewk** |
| hot | sıcak | suh-**jak** |
| cold | soğuk | soh-**ook** |
| good/well | iyi | ee-**yee** |
| bad | kötü | kur-**tew** |
| open | acık | a-**chuhk** |
| closed | kapalı | ka-pa-**luh** |
| left | sol | sol |
| right | sağ | saa |
| near | yakın | ya-**kuhn** |
| far | uzak | oo-**zak** |
| up | yukarı | yoo-ka-**ruh** |
| down | aşağı | a-shah-**uh** |
| early | erken | er-**ken** |
| late | geç | gech |
| toilets | tuvaletler | too-va-let-**ler** |

## Shopping

| | | |
|---|---|---|
| How much is this? | Bu kaç lira? | boo **kach** lee-ra |
| I would like | İstiyorum | ees-**tee**-yo-room |
| Do you have? | Var mı? | **var** muh |
| Do you take credit cards? | Kredi kartı kabul ediyor musunuz? | kreh-dee **kar**-tuh ka-bool eh-**dee**-yor moo-soo-nooz |
| What time do you open/ close? | Saat kaçta açılıyor/ kapanıyor? | Sa-**at** kach-**ta** a-chuh-**luh**-yor/ ka-pa-**nuh**-yor |
| this one | bunu | boo-**noo** |
| that one | şunu | shoo-**noo** |
| expensive | pahalı | pa-ha-**luh** |
| cheap | ucuz | oo-**jooz** |
| size (clothes) | beden | beh-**den** |
| size (shoes) | numara | noo-ma-**ra** |
| white | beyaz | bay-**yaz** |
| black | siyah | see-**yah** |
| red | kırmızı | kuhr-muh-**zuh** |
| yellow | sarı | sa-**ruh** |
| green | yeşil | yeh-**sheel** |
| blue | mavi | ma-**vee** |
| brown | kahverengi | kah-veh-ren-gee |
| shop | dükkan | dewk-**kan** |
| That's my last offer | Daha fazla eremem | da-ha **faz**-la veh-**reh**-mem |

## Types of Shop

| | | |
|---|---|---|
| antiques shop | antikacı | an-**tee**-ka-juh |
| bakery | fırın | fuh-**ruhn** |
| bank | banka | **ban**-ka |
| bookshop | kitapçı | kee-tap-**chuh** |
| cake shop | pastane | pas-ta-**neh** |
| chemist's/ pharmacy | eczane | ej-za-**neh** |
| greengrocer's | manav | ma-**nav** |
| leather shop | derici | deh-ree-**jee** |
| market/bazaar | çarşı/pazar | char-**shuh**/po-**zar** |
| newsstand | gazeteci | ga-**zeh**-teh-jee |
| post office | postane | pos-ta-**neh** |
| shoe shop | ayakkabıcı | eye-**yak**-ka-buh-juh |
| supermarket | süpermarket | sew-per-mar-**ket** |
| tailor | terzi | ter-**zee** |
| travel agency | seyahat acentesi | say-ya-**hat** a-jen-teh-**see** |

## Sightseeing

| | | |
|---|---|---|
| castle | hisar | hee-**sar** |
| church | kilise | kee-**lee**-seh |
| mosque | cami | **ja**-mee |
| museum | müze | **mew**-zeh |
| palace | saray | sar-**eye** |
| park | park | park |
| square | meydan | may-**dan** |
| information office | danışma bürosu | da-nuhsh-**mah** **bew**-ro-soo |
| Turkish bath | hamam | ha-**mam** |

## Transport

| | | |
|---|---|---|
| airport | havalimanı | ha-**va**-lee-ma-nuh |
| bus/coach | otobüs | o-to-**bewss** |
| bus stop | otobüs durağı | o-to-**bewss** doo-**ra**-uh |